# Masters of cinema

# Ethan and Joel Coen

CAHIERS DU
CINEMA

Ian Nathan

# Contents

**5**    **Introduction**

**7**    **Crimewave**
From *Blood Simple* to *Miller's Crossing*

**25**    **The shadow of Hollywood**
From *Barton Fink* to *The Hudsucker Proxy*

**39**    **The unlikeliest heroes**
From *Fargo* to *O Brother, Where Art Thou?*

**57**    **The strangest villains**
From *The Man Who Wasn't There* to *The Ladykillers*

**71**    **The sublime and the ridiculous**
From *No Country for Old Men* to *Burn After Reading*

**83**    **Predictably unpredictable**
From *A Serious Man* to *True Grit*

**98**    Chronology

**100** Filmography

**102** Selected Bibliography

Frances McDormand in *Fargo* (1996).

# Introduction

Joel and Ethan Coen make for awkward interview subjects. They are not difficult or stubborn so much as incapable of offering any meaning to their work. 'It's only a film!' they protest. We are only supposed to watch their films. Hopefully, enjoy them. These two unlikely brothers from a Minneapolis suburb are amiably vague, apologetic, and frequently economic with the truth. Be it their self-effacing Minnesotan natures, or a determination to maintain the mystique that encircles them like mist, they prove allergic to all forms of enquiry and adulation. Two brothers so alike cast and crew swear they share a telepathic link. They just don't think in terms of themes, motifs and latent meaning. Even though, since their auspicious debut in 1984, they have retained final cut and worked unwaveringly from their own scripts, making an indelible mark on American cinema.

Contradiction is an axiom of the Coen technique. The brothers have restless, magpie natures, picking over their favourite books and films, with a predilection for the worms of noir. Voice-overs, dream sequences and surreal comedy are grist to their mill, where the collision of unlikely ideas or images excites them. They have drawn criticism as frigid postmodernists, but there is heart, it's just buried deep. Order and chaos, rules and transgression, God and science: their films flirt with big questions, even as they mock the pretensions of art. They are themselves a contradiction, filmmakers who straddle the independent scene and studio system, but belonging to neither. Theirs is an alternative America built of bloodshed, mythology, irony and genre, often located in provincial hinterlands off Hollywood's radar. Their films also come seasoned with the Coens' own experiences: the listless dog days and bitter winters of their youth, the rituals of Judaism, and a sense of being outsiders in a hybrid nation. This unique alloy of literary and cinematic reference, high style, autobiography and an autopsy on the human predicament is often labelled as Coenesque. If this book has a purpose, it is a quest to identify 'Coenesque', by divining answers from a body of work where the very elusiveness of answers is a theme, and the creators are saying nothing.

Ethan Coen and Joel Coen on the set of *Fargo* (1996).

# Crimewave

From *Blood Simple* to *Miller's Crossing*

Albert Finney in
*Miller's Crossing* (1990).

Following pages: Joel Coen
on the set of *Blood Simple* (1984).

## The Zeimers years

If we are to believe Joel and Ethan Coen, St. Louis Park was an unremarkable place to grow up. Yet its presence can be felt across their films. Named after a local railroad, this failed boomtown has accepted its place as an inert suburbia of Minneapolis. If you require a visual idea of this flat, languid neighbourhood, watch *A Serious Man*. Joel was born on 29 November 1954 with hair that grew long and dark; Ethan on 21 September 1957 with hair that grew frizzy and orange. Their father, Edward, known as Ed, was a professor of economics at the University of Minnesota; their mother, Rena, was a professor of fine arts at St. Cloud State University. They have an older sister, Deborah, now a doctor in Israel, but her place in their history gathers no more significance than the time she spent locked in the bathroom 'washing her hair'.

While obviously bright, neither Coen proved exceptional at school. Ethan might have shown an early inclination for writing at elementary school with a play about King Arthur, and one of their first joint creative ventures was a newspaper, *The Flag Street Sentinel*, sold for two cents a copy (it lasted two issues), but Joel and Ethan had an inauspicious but satisfactory education, and their father didn't hold high hopes for either son. They were regular kids, innately suburban, and mostly bored. The oddity and violence of their films is often seen as a reaction to the ordinariness of their youth, evidence that they are still compensating for spending their seminal winters in the United States' equivalent of Siberia (cue: *Fargo*).

Despite sharing a room, 'Joe' and 'Eth' weren't particularly close, but what they did share was an emerging love of watching films. Their adult counterparts like to smirk that their movie education was a television anthology of Dean Jones's Disney movies (the Herbie series), Tarzan adventures, Jerry Lewis comedies, and anything with Doris Day, Tony Curtis or Bob Hope. Sunny, platitudinous nonsense. But they are unreliable narrators of their own story, retrofitting their formative years to throw journalists off the scent. Evidentially they possess a deep and detailed knowledge of cinema history. At high school they attended the Eight And A Half Club, a film society where their forward-thinking teacher showed them François Truffaut's *The 400 Blows* (1959). Gradually, they became versed in film. Not with the cinephile passion of Martin Scorsese or Truffaut, but the ravenous habits of starving teens. Part of a slow accretion of pop culture unmediated by class or intellectualism, filling their minds with a clutter of films, books, magazines, music, science, history, and a sense of their own ethnic identity.

They hold no snobbery; if anything they are defiantly open-minded. Nor are they left-field hipsters, obsessed with mondo-bizarro subsets of cinema and the knee-jerk thrills of the avant-garde. Their tastes are quite classical. Where Quentin Tarantino, to whom they have often been compared, is gregarious, happy to expound for hours on the referential nature of his films, the Coens squirm under scrutiny, trivializing their process to deflect attention. Tarantino's work declares itself proudly, a recirculation of his off-centre inspirations; the Coens reinvent their favourite films and books in mysterious new guises. Their abiding motivation is the need to please one another. Not that those junior Coens were isolated — they hung out in a gaggle of indolent youngsters who congregated on the sofa in the Coens' basement den. Among them, Ron Neter should take his bow as the founder of Coenesque. It was he who suggested they buy a camera and make some films, raising the cash by mowing neighbourhood lawns. As Neter, now an ad producer in Los Angeles, was to recall, their biggest difficulty was convincing Joel to get off the sofa and get mowing. Finally, they obtained a Vivitar Super 8 camera. So began the primary, and most productive, stage of the Coens' film career. Joel, being the one who went into the shop to buy the camera, thought of himself as director, and having worked out how to switch it on, began playing around with the construction of shots, lying on his back filming his friends leaping out of trees or descending a playground slide.

It was Zeimers who took things to the next level. Before Cage, Clooney and Bridges there was Mark Zimering, known as 'Zeimers': the Coens' first muse. With a thatch of curly-black hair and braces, Zeimers was hardly a conventional leading man. He was simply the most willing and, on camera, charismatic. As they didn't know any girls, Ethan, outfitted in his sister's tutu, would fill in as leading lady. What came out of the Zeimers years was both a charming set of proto-films, and a revealing hint of what was to come. For instance, they were more than happy to borrow from other films: *Zeimers In Zambezi* (shot around 1970) was a loose remake of Cornel Wilde's *The Naked Prey* (1966), while *Ed… A Dog* (the first of many appropriations of their father's name),

their *Lassie Come Home* (1943), had Zeimers bring an unwanted dog home to his parents, played by Neter and Ethan wearing a tutu and inexplicably banging a bongo. None of these films quite captured the primordial Coen aesthetic as does *The Banana Film*, a surrealist episode to be watched while listening to Frank Zappa's *Hot Rats* album. This was Zeimers' final Coen movie, in which he plays a vagrant with a talent for sniffing out bananas. After Ethan, in a tutu, is thrown out of the front door and dies of a heart attack facedown in the snow, Zeimers sniffs out a banana hidden on his body. Having gobbled it down, he clutches his stomach and vomits. The vomit had been carefully concocted beforehand from ingredients from Rena's kitchen and Joel did a lingering close-up. There were no boyish heroics

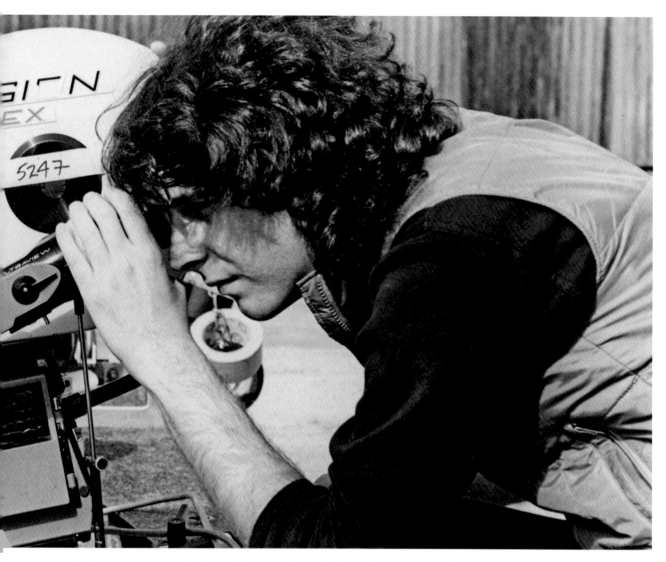

or fantasy stereotypes in these films, rather a dark humour and attention to grotesque detail. They hinted at elusive significance.

It was Joel who would pursue filmmaking at college, taking the undergraduate film studies programme at New York University (august NYU alumni Martin Scorsese and Oliver Stone attended the more renowned postgraduate course). He would return to old, negligent habits, doing little but sit at the back of the class, a grin fixed on his face. For want of anything else, Ethan took philosophy at Princeton. It's tempting to divine significance from the brothers' separate choices: the confluence of filmmaking know-how and philosophical reflection, but they would snort at the notion. After all, Ethan proved an equally indifferent student,

dropping out after a year and re-applying only to discover he was too late. In a burst of absurdist creativity, the younger Coen explained his arm had been blown off in a hunting accident, and was readmitted only after seeing the college psychiatrist. After he graduated in 1979, Ethan moved in with his brother on Riverside Drive on the West Side of Manhattan, and they got to know one another again.

## Methodology

As with so many facets of the bipartite world of the Coens, the specifics of why they chose to join forces remain elusive. They may not be entirely sure themselves; it just seemed the natural thing to do. The likeliest explanation is that with film-student Joel eager to make a foray into directing, he turned to

9

his brother as the more adept writer to help him concoct a screenplay. As the shorthand goes, Joel is the more visual of the two, Ethan the literary one. We shouldn't put too much stock in the distinction. As Frances McDormand explained, it was a smooth, rolling process.[1] Together they are the *auteurs* of their canon. That for the first half of their career Joel was called director and Ethan producer was a way of psychologically ring-fencing their process: they didn't want to be burdened with a meddlesome producer who wasn't blessed by being a Coen brother. Otherwise, any division of labour was entirely 'arbitrary'. They simply share the same fundamental point of view towards the material.

That material is predicated by the words. The camerawork, design, music and acting all serve the ironclad diktats of the page. Right from the beginning came this emphasis on script. Their first film had to be something more than a quick, easy calling card with which to make a name at the studios. Thus they circumvented the cheap thrills of the horror genre, and pursued the heavier demands of crime. In particular the novels of James M. Cain, most celebrated for *Double Indemnity*, *Mildred Pierce* and *The Postman Always Rings Twice*. One of the founding fathers of the aesthetic of film noir,[2] Cain's hardboiled novels are characterized by their earthy settings and sexually charged plotlines where ordinary men are the dupes. Alongside Raymond Chandler and Dashiell Hammett, Cain would complete a trio of pivotal literary inspirations. *Blood Simple*, the title of their first screenplay, which they started writing in 1980, was lifted from Hammett's *Red Harvest* (1929), where the detective hero frets that he too might succumb to the brain fever that afflicts those who have murdered, "If I don't get away soon I'll be going blood-simple like the natives."[3]

*Blood Simple* was borrowing from the same sources as the directors of classic noir, which the Coens supposed made their film noir too. Their methodology was cast in stone from the first: utilizing (and reinventing) pre-existing conventions, the fixtures and fittings of the genre, to tell a unique story. Their films would be aware of the history of film, but as a secondary source. Principally, the screenplay of *Blood Simple* was Cain's throbbing machinations replayed in a contemporary context. Why Texas? Joel had spent a postgraduate year there and Ethan had visited; it was a non-unionized state, cutting down their costs; and, vitally, the landscape possessed a mythical resonance. A place where stories happen.

## The other brothers

The budget for this swirl of wickedness and coal-black humour was estimated at $1.5 million. Paltry in the grand schemes of studio hauteur, but for a pair of unknown brothers from Minnesota, who could barely muster a smile let alone a meeting, it looked insurmountable. Two other offbeat personalities would provide the solution, similarly individualistic spirits who took on the guise of surrogate Coen brothers.

Detroit-born Sam Raimi, future director of the Spider-Man trilogy, was fanatical about making a horror movie. Raimi had funded a provisional thirty-minute version of his maniacal debut *The Evil Dead*, on which he had been working since 1978, by wheedling $380,000 from a procession of Detroit's dentists and lawyers. Three years later, in 1981, he would complete the full 16mm feature, with the assistance of Joel in the edit suite. It was he, and producing partner Robert Tapert, who suggested the Coens borrow the funds for *Blood Simple* from those old neighbourhoods outside of Minneapolis.

Above: Sam Raimi on the set of Sam Raimi's *Evil Dead* (1981).

Opposite page: Joel Coen and Ethan Coen on the set of *Raising Arizona* (1987).

As he had mowed lawns to finance his first camera, Joel trawled door to door, selling the opportunity to invest in a movie at $5,000 to $10,000 a throw (Ethan remained in New York working).

To enhance what was a tough sell to this conservative suburb, Joel came equipped with a two-minute trailer for the film, made with the help of a young cameraman named Barry Sonnenfeld. He would go on to become a successful mainstream director, adding a touch of Coen-flavoured subversion to *The Addams Family* and *Men in Black* movies. First, in dire need of employment, he decided he was a cameraman. His sole qualification, like the teen Coens, being that he had saved up to buy his own Super 8. This led to a series of industrial films, documentaries, and two salutary ventures into the porn industry. Having regretfully hired Joel as the worst assistant he has ever known, Sonnenfeld was enlisted by Joel to shoot the trailer of a (so far) non-existent film. The footage was impressive: gunshots pierce a wall and light filters through and a man is seen being buried alive — shots that would end up in the finished film. Sonnenfeld would become cinematographer on the first three Coen films, helping to define the visual excitement of their early years. Over a painful nine months, Joel had raised $750,000 from the wealthy patrons of St. Louis Park, and $550,000 from smaller investors (including Ed and Rena Coen). The daunting experience of being presented to some local patriarch behind a voluminous desk would leave its mark. Throughout the Coens' films, self-important, often-blustering men appear sat behind desks the size of fortresses.

### The devil in a canary-yellow suit

*Blood Simple* starts with a voice-over: 'The fact is, nothin' comes with a guarantee.' Welcome to *Blood Simple* (1984). Welcome to Coenesque. The mix of novelistic self-interrogation, humour and thriller is set, but this isn't pastiche so much as a paradox, a film both genuinely nasty and ironic — comic noir. That said, the voice-over is swiftly dispensed with.

Dan Hedaya and M. Emmet Walsh in *Blood Simple* (1984).

Loren Visser isn't omniscient; he is soon a participant in the nefarious events, and merely prescribes a mood for us (but from where?). The Coens actively sought out the character actor M. Emmet Walsh to play Visser, having loved him as the sleazy parole officer in Ulu Grosbard's *Straight Time* (1978) with Dustin Hoffman. Walsh agreed, fascinated by this devil in a canary-yellow suit who drives a beaten-up Volkswagen Beetle, spouts Reaganite maxims and laughs like a jackal. He was only slowly won over by the Coens, however — once he was sure there were some wealthy parents putting up the money.

John Getz, by comparison, is wan and dreary as Ray. Taking the trope of the silent type rather too literally, he backs humourlessly into the straight-man role, outpaced by both Walsh and Dan Hedaya, who livens up 'Greek' Marty with his frantic line deliveries and unhinged stare. Marty is the first incarnation of those desk-bound power brokers, a dim but venal villain outmanoeuvred by the waspish Visser. Although concerned by the film's slender budget, Frances McDormand went to the audition to be confronted, in her words, by two geeks much too young to make a movie. By the end of the shoot she had entered into a relationship with Joel, although she claims her rather dumbfounded performance as Abby was a matter of the sheer shock at being cast. [4]

Once they were shooting, *Blood Simple* would be finely calculated, with Sonnenfeld's wide-angle lenses key to the nascent look. Everything in the shot has equal value, leaving it up to the perpetually roaming camera to direct your attention to what is important. If Joel's beloved Stanley Kubrick used wide-angle lenses to alienate the viewer, the Coens use them to bring the watcher in extreme close-up to the action. At times the film has the heady rush of Raimi's *The Evil Dead*: hurtling tracking shots and squeals of violence that shock the slow-burning noir like a burst of electricity. Also unveiled is the Coen talent for a sustained set piece. In this case, a Grand Guignol device born out of Edgar Allan Poe and Hitchcock's famously protracted murder

M. Emmet Walsh and Frances McDormand on the set of *Blood Simple* (1984).

Frances McDormand and Dan Hedaya in *Blood Simple* (1984).

film nor mainstream. How were they to sell that? It was Circle Films, a small distributor based out of Washington, D.C., who picked up *Blood Simple*. Its top man, Ben Barenholtz, hadn't been as impressed by a first film since David Lynch's *Eraserhead* (1977) and signed the Coens up on a four-picture deal. The film made enough of a splash in film circles to have both Steven Spielberg and Hugh Hefner invite the brothers over. They turned the contrasting temptations down.

### Trailer trash

On its modest scale, *Blood Simple* made money, and those brave Minnesotan investors would see a return of 150 per cent. Meanwhile, the Coens moved into a new, if hardly salubrious, office on New York's West 23rd Street. It was here, while munching on doughnuts and making coffee on the stove, that they turned their thoughts to their next film. They had one clear motivation, a career motto borrowed from Monty Python: now for something completely different. After the shadowy games of *Blood Simple* they were intent on a much faster pace and a lighter tone. In fact, the work would evolve into a comic maelstrom inspired by the manic invention of Chuck Jones's Road Runner cartoons. Their characters would, pejoratively, be trailer trash. Their setting would be the cacti-spotted desert highways of Arizona (a further nod to the woebegone efforts of Wile E. Coyote to catch that pesky bird). And their central plot device, most bizarrely, would be a baby. As neither brother was yet a father, the attraction was that of a foreign experience — as murder had been with their debut, Ethan hastened to add.[7]

Viewed in hindsight, *Raising Arizona* (1987) looks less of a departure than it appeared at the time. Seeking out another pocket of American life, indeed playing on rural stereotypes (as we shall see, controversially), with elements of botched crime and slapstick, have become familiar refrains. By a rudimentary division, Coen films can be split into the more searching noir thrillers and the sunnier, screwball (but still noir-derived) comedies; similar to Howard Hawks's vacillating tastes (Hawks was famed for making a film in every genre, without losing what was essentially Hawksian about them). The latter variation on Coenesque began with *Raising Arizona*, which used a hyperkinetic comic aesthetic to create a homily to family values.

scene in *Torn Curtain* (1966). Ray, thinking Abby has shot her husband, attempts to dispose of the body only to discover he is not entirely deceased. Over a wordless and horribly hilarious nine minutes, Ray attempts to bury an unwilling Marty. In the wide shot, the body squirming beneath the dirt is actually Ethan's. Roads disappear into midnight, electric fly traps crackle hungrily, and the plot contorts itself deliciously, throwing each character into his or her version of events (misunderstanding a reality only the audience fully grasp). Everyone is in the dark, so to speak.

When the film was screened at festivals (Deauville, Toronto, Sundance), critics warmed to its subtle bending but not breaking of the rules, its genuflection but not slavery to the props of noir. At *New York* magazine, David Denby thrilled to how 'self-assured' these young directors were.[5] Whereas Pauline Kael, doyenne of *The New Yorker*, became the first of many to judge the Coens as all gesture and allusion, rather than the real thing: 'it comes on self-mocking, but it has no self to mock'.[6]

The brothers were more concerned with finding a distributor. Another schlep was required for the footsore Joel, this time selling his wares to Hollywood. On their introduction to Coenesque, the majors were baffled. *Blood Simple* seemed neither art

The budget quadrupled from *Blood Simple*'s $1.5 million to $6 million, and Circle Films, who had raised an initial $3 million, turned to 20th Century Fox to provide the rest, albeit without them having any say in the film. It was Scott Rudin, then executive vice-president of Fox, who agreed to the deal.

## Once upon a time in America

After Kevin Costner turned them down, the Coens asked Nicolas Cage to play Hi, an inveterate petty crook with a habit of robbing dime stores wearing a stocking mask. Topped with a hank of uncontrollable Woody-Woodpecker hair, and a shocking array of shirts, his ungainly body language and melancholy diction give Hi a charming vulnerability. But Cage, who enjoyed exploring Method acting, wanted to improvise and found himself hemmed in by the strictures of the Coen method. He later described his directors as 'autocratic'. In contrast, they had written Ed, the duty cop assigned to take Hi's mug shot every time he's arrested, and with whom he falls in love, for Holly Hunter, who having shared a flat with Frances McDormand as a student, had become a close friend (Hunter had also

been their first choice for Abby in *Blood Simple*). The actress loved the idea that Ed was a natural disciplinarian surrounded by misbehaving men. The oafish shapes of John Goodman and William Forsythe filled the grotesque Snoats brothers, who break out of prison seemingly only to lure their old prison buddy Hi back beyond the bounds of the law. For Nathan Arizona, the voluble furniture salesman and the father of the baby that Hi and Ed decide to raise when they learn that they can't have children of their own, they found the ebullient Texan actor Trey Wilson. For the all-important quintuplets, an open casting call was held in Scottsdale, Arizona, where they saw more than 400 tots, and cast 15 on the basis of 'not crying when mommy went away'. One poor baby was fired for learning to walk. For Nathan Jr., the stolen sprog, they found T. J. Kuhn, possibly the most even-tempered and compliant child in the whole of Arizona. As far as the brothers were concerned, he was the perfect actor. There was just room for a small role for McDormand as the gauche Dot, wife of Hi's boss, mother to a ill-tempered brood, and source of unwelcome dispatches of child-rearing advice.

Nicolas Cage in *Raising Arizona* (1987).

Randall 'Tex' Cobb in *Raising Arizona* (1987).

For all its randomness, the Coenesque universe has a moral gravity. All crimes, even well-meaning ones, will spiral out of control. As soon as Hi purloins Nathan Jr. the forces of chaos descend upon him and Ed — farcical circumstances that will reach an appointed cartoon frenzy of chase scenes constructed from crashing zooms and tracking shots. The Coens also mixed in western elements: horse pursuits re-envisioned with cars and motorbikes, with the Snoats brothers clad in Sergio Leone-style trail duster coats. Given the deep-grained inertia of their Midwestern personalities, their new set of characters initiated a readiness to depict their exact opposite. *Raising Arizona* discharges a barrage of highly strung feelings. Hunter's fusillade of tears upon first hugging Nathan Jr. is a wonder to behold. In a theme that would play across the Coens' career, it is the adults, mostly men, who are infantile. None of the babies sheds a tear, while the grown-up cast don't just sob, they bellow, and nigh on ululate their frustrations. This is a once-upon-a-time America where people grow younger on the inside. An America that is treading a thin line.

Getting hold of the script, a Tempe newspaper was dismayed at the portrayal of locals, and some critics judged it condescending. The characters' exaggerated dialect was based on the regional accent and a notion of what they, particularly Hi, might be reading, namely: supermarket magazines and the Bible. The voice-over exemplifies this florid style. Filled with folksy wisdom, its seeds events with a mock-lyrical idiom ('More and more my thoughts turned to Ed, and I finally felt the pain of imprisonment'). Ethan defended their approach as deliberately inaccurate; this was an Arizona of the mind and a pastiche of John Steinbeck's parochial fiction, and the eclectic communities of William Faulkner and Flannery O'Connor's South. All those misguided dreams of small Americans. The Lone Biker of the Apocalypse, a hellish figure conjured by Hi and Ed's dishonesty, is named Leonard Smalls in reference to *Of Mice and Men*'s unfortunate

Nicolas Cage and Holly Hunter in *Raising Arizona* (1987).

man-child Lennie Small. The overall tenor is that of a wired folktale, or a Preston Sturges comedy played at a delirium. An eclectic cocktail made ever fizzier by ingredients from *Bringing Up Baby*, *Bonnie and Clyde* and *Fellini's Roma*. The Lone Biker arrives on a dented Harley-Davidson, blasting basking lizards from boulders: a messenger from George Miller's post-apocalyptic action movie *Mad Max 2: The Road Warrior* (1981). Filled by the alarming frame of ex-boxer Randall 'Tex' Cobb, this satanic emissary proved a headache. Not least, because Cobb couldn't handle the motorcycle, often missing his mark and ruining the take. He didn't take too kindly to direction either. Promoting the film, Joel flinched at Cobb's mention, suggesting they were in no great hurry to cast him again.

## Looney tunes

What is apparent in *Raising Arizona* is how the unorthodox camerawork, far from showing off, is an extension of the Coen vernacular. There is a dialogue at work: jokes with corresponding punch-lines, visual rhymes, a rhetoric as honed as the Coens' screenplays. When a gurgling baby nods its head we switch to his POV, the camera bobbing at an identical rate. Where Hi pulls an escaping quintuplet from beneath the cot by his tootsies, he is dragged by his feet from under a car by the Lone Biker. To manage this anarchic language, the storyboarding needed to be clinically precise. The Coens would map out their film virtually frame by frame, efficiently controlling the budget in the process. To do this they formed a pivotal creative partnership with storyboard artist J. Todd Anderson, who has since worked on all their films.

Propelled by composer Carter Burwell's squall of folksy elements (banjo, choir, whistling and yodelling, plus excerpts of Beethoven's Ninth), *Raising Arizona* is best recalled for its 'fast-forward' tracking shots. Steadicam being far too smooth and expensive for the film's scruffiness, the Coens appropriated Raimi's homemade tracking shots from *The Evil*

*Dead*, christened Shakicam. This amounted to fixing the camera to a wooden plank and have two grips run along with it, reaching a crescendo when Florence Arizona (Lynne Dumin Kitei), the quintuplets' mother, discovers one of her tots is missing and the camera hurtles down streets, through car windows, and up a ladder, to her face's screaming mouth in extreme close-up. Amid such hysteria the low rumble of political satire is sometimes missed.

Coen films don't readily suggest political contexts; they exist in a parallel universe to real events, where history can be heard only faintly. Race and religion have a stronger influence on the Coens, determining how they position characters in society or culture (Jews as self-regarding intellectuals, Southern 'hicks' as strugglers). Most markedly, the Coens take issue with capitalism: money and those that wield its power (the Arizonas, for example) are seen as crass or villainous. Those that pursue the American Dream will be dashed against the rocks of their own scheming. Here in the 1980s, Reaganite advancement smells sour. *Blood Simple*'s Loren Visser sneers that even if you are Man of the Year 'something can always go wrong', and these unlikely denizens of *Raising Arizona* are stuck on Reaganomics' lowliest rung. Hi's light-fingered addictions are a perverse form of consumerism, and in Nathan Arizona's recourse to hard sell at every opportunity, the Coens are attacking the way Americans wrap up morality in advertising slogans. With some irony then, *Raising Arizona* became a smash hit, making $22 million in the USA. And Hollywood, Reagan's former employer, became ever more curious about these peculiar brothers.

### A 'dirty town movie'

Having toyed with the conventions of genre, the Coens were eager to immerse themselves entirely in a made-up world. To explore a genre from the inside. Given their leaning towards crime stories, enshrined in book and film, they hit upon the gangster movie as the perfect milieu. One in the vein of the Warner Brothers thrillers of the 1930s, set in a Prohibition-era America dominated by Al Capone and his cronies, who ruled their cities through an inverted moral code. But there would be strictly no external references to real history — the Coens didn't even want to give their city a name. As the succinct title card to *Miller's Crossing* (1990) informs us, the film takes place in 'An Eastern city in the

United States, toward the end of the 1920s'. They would build a finely nuanced but unspecific 'movie space'. Joel liked to call it their 'dirty town movie'.

And with Coenesque deviance, the film's complex plot was to be driven not by the auspices of James Cagney films *per se*, but by an existential anti-hero straight out of a Dashiell Hammett novel. To be precise, they were liberating — cynics might say appropriating — entire plot devices from *The Glass Key* (1931) and *Red Harvest* (1929). One of the great pleasures of *Miller's Crossing* is that neither Hammett's noir nor the gangster thriller hold sway. As a more luxuriant $11 million undertaking, it required studio backing, but the success of *Raising Arizona* had left them in good stead with 20th Century Fox. Circle Films remained as co-producers, and Ben Barenholtz brokered a deal with the studio based on a frankly baffling two-line description: gangland boss Leo O'Bannon discovers his best friend and right-hand man Tom Reagan is having an affair with his girl, Verna Bernbaum, just as rival boss Johnny Caspar makes his move to take over the city. Verna truly loves Tom, but wants Leo to protect her brother Bernie, who has been selling out Johnny's fixed fights, while Tom is ultimately out to protect Leo.

## Lost in translation

Until now, writing scripts had been relatively painless. The Coens' process was simple: Ethan typed on their Smith Corona electric typewriter, while Joel paced or slouched across the sofa in their New York office. From each nascent image or phrase, they would try things out, see if they made them laugh, and a framework would emerge. This way they got to know their worlds, feel them, wending their way to the finale. However, halfway through *Miller's Crossing* they became stuck, and it would take eight painful months to complete. They insist writer's block is too strong a term for what happened, but the plot had become impossibly entangled. They decided a change of scene was required. Decamping to the Los Angeles apartment of friend William Preston Robertson, they sat around, ate doughnuts and watched *Jeopardy!* on television. If anything, they were regressing. In search of fresh air, they went out to see *Baby Boom* (1987) starring Diane Keaton, latest in a line of tedious infant-themed comedies that

Albert Finney and Gabriel Byrne in *Miller's Crossing* (1990).    19

John Turturro in *Miller's Crossing* (1990).

Gabriel Byrne, Tony Sirico and Harry Bugin in *Miller's Crossing* (1990).

had followed in the wake of *Raising Arizona*. Did it recall the easy climate of writing their desert comedy? Or simply convince them not to take things so seriously? Whatever it was, it worked. They jetted back to New York, and in three weeks had written the first draft of *Barton Fink*, the tale of a nervy Jewish playwright struck down with writer's block while writing a script for a Hollywood studio. Their brains washed out, *Miller's Crossing* came together, and a patient Fox agreed to go ahead.

They had written the role of Irish boss Leo for Trey Wilson, but days before rehearsals were due to begin, the forty-year-old died of a brain aneurysm. With good fortune, veteran British actor Albert Finney agreed to step in. Despite being ten years older than Wilson, not a word of the script was changed, but Finney's presence would bring an interesting shift to the film's dynamics. In Finney's hands, Leo gains pathos. In *Miller's Crossing*, the Coens cast John Turturro for the first time. Although Italian—American, he has adaptable looks and passed easily for this pernicious Jew, to give a powerful performance, fearlessly raw in the film's best remembered sequence where Tom

(Gabriel Byrne) marches him to Miller's Crossing to put a bullet in his brain while he pleads for his life, debasing himself, a man reduced to a pitiful beggar imploring his captor to 'look in your heart'.

The film may have been constructed out of pre-existing forms, pieces of an intricate jigsaw, but it comes alive thanks to the darkly comic performances, not least that of Jon Polito as bombastic Italian hood Johnny, a very Coenesque variety of villain who mistakes talking for thinking.

## A perfect fake

To achieve the film's princely look, Barry Sonnenfeld convinced them to use long lenses over the muscular wide-angle variety. The camera would glide forwards, relishing the sophisticated production design. Having rejected San Francisco as faux period, they shot in New Orleans, whose resistance to gentrification had left many districts unchanged since the 1920s. This may be an archetypal setting, but it is never conscious of its own artifice. A fine balance is held between a gripping realism and a comic-book fantasy of crooks in heavy coats fast-talking in an absurd yet believable criminal argot.

The film claims a solemnity almost despite itself: the perfect fake.

The directors refine the manic set pieces of *Raising Arizona* into meticulously choreographed violence, most vividly when Leo turns the tables on a pair of assassins. This unforgettable shoot marks the point where the gangster movie gravitates towards the lone journey of the existential anti-hero of film noir. Tom slips out of his own time, to take on the guise of Alain Delon's Le Samouraï and the smart-talking Bogartian icon of *The Big Sleep* or *The Maltese Falcon*. Raymond Chandler's influence works its way into the labyrinthine plot, its near incomprehensibility an extension of the film's texture.

While being a contraption built from stereotypes, *Miller's Crossing* has such compositional care that it escapes its own trap; the brothers' style borders on a self-anointed classicism. The palate has the rich, honeyed lustre of the whiskey Tom takes in a single swallow (drinking allowed a man to think according to Hammett). Dennis Gassner's production design matches the cinematography: a luxurious tableau of wood panelling and leather, the rooms sweeping back for ever, as they do in *Citizen Kane*. Apart from a single

# The Thompson Jitterbug

Within their multidimensional plots, the Coens have a gift for the singular moment. Snowglobe Coen movies in perfect miniature: here lies a microcosm of their process, reshuffling the formulaic into meaningful new forms. Take *Miller's Crossing*'s Thompson Jitterbug, the classic gangster shoot-out turned into the quintessential Coen action scene.

The brothers awarded this sequence its nickname after the hood who, strafed with submachine gunfire, dances like a marionette. We catch the muzzle flash of his Thompson circling the room like a crazed Ferris wheel, and blowing his own toes off. But this is merely one facet of what conventionally is a shoot-out, before the Coens coat it in black comedy, exploration of character and the diegetic use of music. The sequence begins with a gramophone needle lowered onto the swooning elegy of 'Danny Boy', re-recorded especially for the film by Irish tenor Frank Patterson, giving the scene a wicked irony with its plaintive, mysterious lyrics. As Ethan Coen explained to *Premiere* magazine in 1990, while not designed as necessarily funny, the scene was meant to be fun. It was also important, however flamboyant their plans, that the

action didn't break the spell of *Miller's Crossing*'s composed gangster aesthetic.

The Jitterbug marks the point that Johnny Caspar (Jon Polito), head of the Italian faction, makes explicit his attempts to take over the city by dispatching assassins to the home of Irish boss Leo O'Bannon (Albert Finney) to eliminate him. Up until now, Leo has appeared an avuncular figure, blindsided by his infatuation with Verna Bernbaum (Marcia Gay Harden). This sequence serves as a dramatic demonstration of the skills that elevated him to top dog. 'It was the point', Ethan noted with relish, 'to shed a little blood.'

Once the melody crackles into life, a tracking shot glides past the body of Leo's bodyguard and into his house. The camera's movement is fluent, radically sophisticated compared to the 'Shakicam' moves of *Raising Arizona*. We notice, in passing, the bodyguard's cigarette set light to a newspaper. The actual house was in New Orleans' French Quarter, a signal of Leo's wealth and position. We cut to Leo stubbing out his cigar (a visual rhyme to the cigarette) before a zephyr of smoke rising through the floorboards catches his attention. Leo is intercut with the two

assassins climbing the stairs, their steps in perfect unison foreshadowing the concept of a 'dance'.

As the gunmen burst through the door we catch Leo grabbing a revolver and scrambling beneath his bed. The killers begin filling the room with gunfire and we cut to Leo's point of view from beneath the bed, an angle that necessitated elevating the set by three feet. It is a hallmark of the Coens' style that they consider the dynamics of action with as severe exactitude as they do almost everything else, discovering a wit and originality. A crack shot, Leo hits one of his assailants in the ankle, sending him crashing to the floor, granting a clear shot at his head.

The Coens' mastery of cause and effect is exemplified by the image of white feathers floating in the air. For all its realism, the surreal effect of flying metal and pillow feathers reinforces our sense of being located 'inside' a genre. The entire sequence is as shapely as a well-told anecdote or joke. Significantly, when it finishes, we cut to Lanny Flaherty's Terry (one of Leo's lieutenants) concluding his own account of the previous night's excitement. Have we been inside his version of events all along?

With one opponent down, Leo scoots out, grabbing the dead man's Thompson, and exits out of an open window. With the other gunman now 'framed' in the window, Leo turns the gun on him. The barrage of his bullets striking his body combined with the recoil from his own Thompson makes him dance. The scene concludes with Leo blasting the getaway car, which swerves and hits a tree, bursting into flames as his house burns in the background. At the same time, 'Danny Boy' swells to its mournful crescendo, sentiment colliding with a lethal command of death. In a film run to the 'quick-fire' pace of its dialogue, excepting the song's lyrics, only now do we realize not a word has been spoken.

Albert Finney in *Miller's Crossing* (1990).

Sam Raimi in *Miller's Crossing* (1990).

visit to the boudoir of Leo's club, and even Verna's apartment, these are masculine spaces. Gassner saw Tom's room, sparse yet detailed, as a representation of his headspace: there are inner chambers concealed by sliding doors, and a phone rings like a ripple of anxiety. Over the opening credits we see this hat swept along with the autumn leaves. We later learn it is Tom's dream, and he spends most of the film chasing after his fedora. Byrne himself was desperate to grasp the significance of the film's central motif, but his directors only shrugged — it's just a hat. Is it truly an empty emblem? A joke about the act of symbolism itself? Or a symbol of Tom's quest, the elusive, unknowable prize he seeks? In the perfect final shot, Tom has lost everything but his hat, which he draws down over his eyes. There isn't an answer. As he says to Leo, 'Do you know why you do things?'

*Miller's Crossing* flopped on its release, lost in the early 1990s revival of the gangster genre that, ironically enough, was supposed to insure its chances. Turns out you can't trust a fix. Martin Scorsese's *Goodfellas*, Francis Ford Coppola's *The Godfather Part III* and, later, Barry Levinson's *Bugsy* proved too dominant, and the Coens' entry into the renaissance, despite positive reviews and the honour of opening the New York Film Festival, failed to find an audience. It was their first taste of failure, but time has yielded an honoured place for their most unusually poignant film. Fans admire it as their most complete and handsome work.

# The shadow of Hollywood

## From *Barton Fink* to *The Hudsucker Proxy*

John Turturro in
*Barton Fink* (1991).

Following pages: John Turturro
and John Goodman in *Barton
Fink* (1991).

### Hotel California

Before *Miller's Crossing* had been released, the Coens were well into production on their following picture. This rhythm of overlapping projects was a signature of their early years — a sign of both a confident stream of creativity and a defence against a previous film's failure at the box office. Unlike their peers, the Coens weren't necessarily interested in working with bigger and bigger train sets, only funding the narrative requirements in hand. Some films would cost more, some less. Again backed by a co-production between 20th Century Fox and Circle Films (the final film in their deal with Ben Barenholtz), the rules remained the same: their backers could turn down the script, but the Coens kept final cut. At $9 million no one was breaking into a sweat.

The perplexing story of Barton Fink, celebrated playwright, champion of the common man and flummoxed writer of 'wrestling pictures', had poured out of the Coens in three weeks. They would usually take four months on a first draft. This time they knew exactly where they were headed from the outset. Halfway through *Barton Fink* would be a significant 'turn' of events. But rather than *Miller's Crossing*'s smooth transition into noir, here was a jolt into horror. Alongside *A Serious Man* (2009), *Barton Fink* (1991) is the Coens' most ambiguous yet stimulating film. Drifting in a liminal zone between pitch-black comedy and psychological thriller, this arty bedevilment is probably their most analysed film, even though the Coens implore us that they designed it to be indecipherable. Care of Ethan's droll explanation, it should be viewed merely as 'a boring comedy. Slow-paced. Sort of confused, generically.'[8]

Yet, *Barton Fink* does adhere to a genre, or subgenre, in the Hollywood satire: it is a film about filmmaking. In fact, it is a film about *writing* films. Or trying to. With twisted Coenesque logic, it is writer's block (reflecting their troubles completing *Miller's Crossing*) that propels the plot. Alongside a customary batch of Coen preoccupations: the conflict between art and entertainment, the Jewish condition, visions of damnation, problematic hair, and a psychopathic insurance salesman in the room next door who might be the manifestation of an unravelling mind. Of such things, according to their contrarian spirit, great comedies are made. The initial basis was the book *City of Nets: A Portrait of Hollywood in the 1940's* by Otto Friedrich, an eloquent exploration of the experiences of German expatriates in Los Angeles. Here too was a distillation of

their own early view of the studio system, all its galumphing power and banality, but relocated to a 1941 days before America entered into World War II, the year of *Citizen Kane*, *The Maltese Falcon* and Preston Sturges's *Sullivan's Travels*.

Rather than an idiosyncratic pocket of America, the film is set in Los Angeles, albeit a Los Angeles of the mind, where a playwright turned screenwriter named Barton Fink (John Turturro) will be ensnared by writer's block, his only solace a friendly salesman with a dark secret (John Goodman). The brothers had pictured this huge, dilapidated hotel where Turturro and Goodman sit side by side on a bed in their underwear. This ebullient, sensitive actor, belying his considerable 400-pound bulk, brings energy and bonhomie to their films, but beneath the affability always lurks menace. There could be no greater incongruity to Turturro's snitty, self-involved, mole-like Barton, straining for inspiration, than this brute of a man. Considering we are discussing two brothers working in close proximity, one tall and gangly, the other short and wiry, is there not a warped self-portrait to such double acts? Male bonding and a corresponding set of dysfunctional masculine clans (crooks, gangsters, businessmen, prisoners, lawyers, cowboys and bowlers) are deeply encoded in the Coen mainframe.

## That Barton Fink feeling

*Barton Fink* opens on the playwright standing in the wings of his latest triumph, evidently a Jewish intellectual by way of his heavy glasses, awkward stance and his hair: an upwardly bound pillar of frizzy curls that will grow inexorably through the film. The name of the play — a daft concoction of common folk orating their personal dreams and an early index of Barton's artistic pretensions — is *Bare Ruined Choirs* (lifted from Shakespeare's 73rd Sonnet). Its success will sweep him from Manhattan, and dreams of founding a theatre for the common man, into the ample arms of a common man. Egocentric Barton clings to a notion of artistic purity, planting himself in the dishabille if not diabolic Hotel Earle, way off the studio campus. On one of his few excursions into daylight, Barton meets John Mahoney's W. P. Mayhew, a barely functioning (luridly vomiting) alcoholic screenwriter. In all but name he is William Faulkner, another literary great who took his turn at the Hollywood coalface. His secret is that, as he can barely stand, his elegantly long-suffering assistant Audrey (Judy

Davis) is ghosting him. Could she become a 'ghost-writer' for our nominal hero?

Barton is out of keel with his times. He's dressed for the wrong decade, hunched in a tweed suit, resident of a haunted hotel. As *Miller's Crossing* turned Tom into a Bogart-type, Barton slips out of a specific reality into a mythological space. Coen worlds come refracted through the looking glass of fiction rather than history. Here lie those accusations of ironic distance, even the vice of postmodernism, where feeling is embalmed in the aspic of their cleverness. But the Coens take the structures of their chosen genres and contort them into unexpected shapes in order to reveal truths. America is a society where myth blurs with reality. Of course, they would also claim to be chasing a quick laugh. And in the hands of Michael Lerner, bellowing, barmy Jack Lipnick, head of Capitol Pictures, is the film's comic relief: a hilarious greatest hits package of tyrannical Hollywood moguls. Lipnick is an alternative clichéd Jew of old Hollywood, bending young talent to his will. 'We're only interested in one thing,' he demands, 'can you tell a story?' Barton is commanded to come up with a wrestling picture for real-life boxer-turned-actor Wallace Beery. For the directors, wrestling summed up a crass popularism opposite to Barton's intellectual hooey. Metaphorically, he would be 'wrestling' with his soul. But at the heart of *Barton Fink* is a disdain for artistic pretension. While Barton appears some finicky Coen ancestor (the nerdy Jewish persona, the unruly hair, the uncomfortable place at the Hollywood table), they wave it away. Art? Don't be foolish. Even so, there is no avoiding how the film revels in themes about the search for authenticity.

## The wallpaper movie

The startling look of *Barton Fink*, particularly the dissipated gloom of the Earle, will collude with the clammy textures of horror as much as the Coens' beloved noir. But rather than *Blood Simple*'s jesting, hyperkinetic moves borrowed from Sam Raimi, here they were calling upon the austere power of Roman Polanski and Stanley Kubrick. *The Tenant*

(1976), *Cul-de-sac* (1966) and *Repulsion* (1965) loom large over the Earle, whose long, spectral corridors also pay homage to the Overlook Hotel (another fulcrum of writer's block) of *The Shining* (1980). Like the Overlook, the Earle could be a gateway to Hell. The word 'six' is said three times as Barton ascends in the elevator and at the ringing bell the bellhop Chet (Steve Buscemi) rises up out of a trapdoor. Printed on the hotel notepaper is an invitation to 'Stay a day or a lifetime!' — a dubious offer the Coens had discovered on the stationery of an insalubrious Texan hotel while shooting *Blood Simple*. It didn't go unnoticed that when the film premiered at Cannes, Polanski was head of the jury. *Barton Fink*'s torments would be lavished with the Palme d'Or and Best Director (for Joel) and Best Actor (for Turturro).

With Barry Sonnenfeld departed to direct *The Addams Family*, the Coens had turned to British cinematographer Roger Deakins to fulfil these dank visions, impressed by his work on Mike Figgis's *Stormy Monday* (1988). He swiftly learned to decipher their gnomic instructions and hurdy-gurdy laughs, and has proved equal to their visual exoticism ever since. Deakins posited the notion that Barton's room is a manifestation of the thwarted writer's state of mind. Indeed, the entire climate of the movie reflects his psychological state — unpeeling like the wallpaper. The insistent mosquito is the shrill nag of his conscience. Charlie Meadows the horrific embodiment of his 'common man'. 'I'll show you the life of the mind', bellows Charlie, exposed as the serial killer Karl 'Madman' Mundt (notably of German extraction), stomping down the corridor, trailing fire and damnation in his wake (the building also reflects Charlie's psyche — then he *is* Barton). Again, to the Coens' disgust, it was inferred that Barton's torments are a parable of Jewish victimization, his own Holocaust. This time with better cause: is it arbitrary that the two American-ethnic cops who come for Charlie are Italian and German?

Even as they professed their sole intention was to entertain, the Coens suffered no illusions that their latest film was highly commercial. Too slow and ambiguous to sit well in multiplexes, it was to cleave to the art-house circuit, making $6 million in America (and working its way into profit overseas), despite that Palme d'Or. If it was an entertainment, it was a provocative one, and their growing

body of devoted fans lapped it up. But like Barton, the common man was eluding Joel and Ethan.

### A postmodern joke

'*Hudsucker* truly is a comment on the genre it draws from', admitted Joel,[9] contemplating an even more indifferent public response that was to greet *The Hudsucker Proxy* (1994). A love song to old Hollywood that manages simultaneously to be the Coens' most archly contrived film yet. Artifice is its very meaning, a postmodern joke about being labelled postmodernists. No other film displays the sheer inventory of their gifts to such dazzling extent. No other film keeps the audience at such a remove. Coenesque contradictions run rife, not least of which is that they thought they were following *Barton Fink* with a crowd-pleaser. This high concept they had stored away since 1984, when the

Joel Coen with John Turturro
on the set of *Barton Fink* (1991).

brothers joined forces with Sam Raimi on a screen-play that featured a clueless country boy who rises, with suspicious haste, to the top of a giant corpora-tion. A story embedded within a fantastical, fairy-lit New York on the cusp of 1959. Its ambitions were lavish, requiring multiple special effects and huge Art Deco sets to create this grand edifice of big business. Never has their anti-capitalist theme been writ larger. At that stage in their careers, *The Hudsucker Proxy* was completely beyond them. But after *Barton Fink* they wondered if they could mus-ter the $25 million required to bring to life their first film to be inspired more by a cinematic tra-dition than a literary one. Rather than their holy trinity of crime writers (Cain/Chandler/Hammett) here was a synthesis of their triumvirate of direc-torial heroes: Frank Capra, Howard Hawks and Preston Sturges.

# The secret inspiration for Barton Fink

The Coens claimed any resemblance their bespectacled New York playwright-turned-screenwriter Barton Fink had to real bespectacled New York playwright-turned-screenwriter Clifford Odets was merely in passing, but as usual they were being circumspect. As far as John Turturro was concerned, he was the foremost inspiration for his character and the actor delved deep into the various biographies and Odets' personal diaries to get a full picture of the man behind Fink. After all, the physical resemblance is there for all to see. And you can clearly hear Fink's ironic hyperbole in Odets' vaulting quotes: 'All my boyhood and youth I thought of the word *nobility* and what it meant.'

Born in Philadelphia in 1906 to Russian–Jewish immigrant parents, Odets was one of the founders of the Group Theatre (with Elia Kazan), which pioneered the realist acting methods of Stanislavski and more truthful, politically left-wing subjects, heavily critical of the prevailing capitalist system. In other words, as Barton Fink might put it, a theatre for and of the 'common man', which of course only truly played to the intelligentsia. Odets' most famous plays even sound like Coen jokes: *Waiting for Lefty* (about cab drivers planning a strike, in which the audience becomes part of the meeting) and the production that made him a superstar in 1935, *Awake and Sing!* (tracking an impoverished Bronx family of the 1930s). What we hear of Fink's *Bare Ruined Choirs*, in the opening scene of the film, derisively apes the declarative flourishes of Odets' style: 'But we're part of that choir, both of us – yeah, and you, Maury, and Uncle Dave too!'

However, Odets would make the transition to Hollywood to write for the studios, which rather dented his image as an artist for the people. He would be heavily criticized for never having fulfilled his artistic potential, and always claimed he wanted to return to New York – but he never did. There is little doubt he enjoyed his Hollywood sojourn, working his way through many women (including two marriages), and garnering a reputation for the high life. During the 1940s he wrote the first draft of *It's A Wonderful Life* and formed a close friendship with Jean Renoir, another intellectual immigrant to Hollywood. But as the shadow of McCarthy loomed after World War II, the House Committee on Un-American Activities investigated Odets. Disavowing any communist affiliation, he escaped being blacklisted, and named no names, but the public reacted poorly to his having testified as a 'friendly witness' and he never fully recovered. Kazan felt his voice had been 'choked', but there are threads of his disillusionment in his screenplay for the Coen-favourite *Sweet Smell of Success* in 1957. He would conclude his career on a creatively low but lucrative ebb, writing for television. His last play, *The Flowering Peach*, in 1955, was a Broadway failure. Odets died of colon cancer in 1963 – he was fifty-seven.

John Turturro in *Barton Fink* (1991).

## A Silver lining

Even for their fifth film, raising a budget double anything the Coens had worked with before was a tall order. *Barton Fink* had done marvels for their reputation as artists, but nothing for them as a commercial proposition. Nevertheless, when their agent Jim Berkus suggested he take the script to Joel Silver, a producer of mainstream Hollywood entertainment (*Die Hard*, *Lethal Weapon*, *Predator*), they couldn't help laughing. Silver suggested it might be nice if more than twelve people saw one of them, and went on to convince Warner Brothers this was a chance to get good reviews and a box-office return. The brothers, conscious the studio should recoup their investment, accepted for the first time that they would have to clear casting with their new employers.

All parties agreed that Tim Robbins would be the perfect Norville Barnes, the doltish protagonist cut from Capra's Jimmy Stewart-mould with his big heart and farm-boy innocence, but irredeemably dim. The complex plot has the conniving board of Hudsucker Industries plant this 'numbskull' as their new chairman in order to send the stock spiralling down so they can buy it up cheap. Fate, and irony, will intervene when Barnes invents the hula hoop. Following Robert Altman's biting Hollywood satire *The Player* (1992), Robbins was on something of a career high, and the Coens enjoyed his take on the character as not necessarily dumb, just ill-equipped. Norville suffers from a common Coen ailment: he refuses to listen. He is in a bubble — his own film. Realization is denied him. He's the Proxy, a necessary imbecile, and a vital cog in the apparatus of the film. He is a type of character rather than a character, and, for all Robbins's effervescence and valiant slapstick, one hard to love.

Jennifer Jason Leigh's Amy Archer, was based on Rosalind Russell in Hawks's *His Girl Friday* (1940), Barbara Stanwyck in Sturges's *The Lady Eve* (1941), and Katharine Hepburn in just about everything she did. At times the burden is too much for Leigh. The villain of the piece, much to Warners' satisfaction, was to be played by Paul Newman, who admired the Coens' knack of moving sideways through a story like crabs, but the film leaves him monotone.

## Where style is substance

Despite the swelling budget and special effects, the film is less a departure than a concentration of the Coen aesthetic. How the surfaces sparkle: the boardroom table, reflecting the city like a still lake, was so vast it had to be assembled from five different sections. The Hudsucker Building's upper echelons gleam like marble, reflecting the soullessness of the pursuit of money, the taint of success. This is an alt-America where God struggles with Mammon. Great forces are at work, a battle for Norville's soul. Absolute evil in the guise of a sinister fix-it man (Harry Bugin) scratching names from doors, eradicating them from the record, and Bill Cobbs's Moses as the representative of good, the wise clock-keeper whose lilting voice-over prescribes him as storyteller. He's another layer of make-believe addressing a world outside the world of the film. We couldn't be more aware we are watching a film. Style and theme are indivisible.

Evoking the magnitude of *Citizen Kane*, the sets were built across the Carolco Studios in Wilmington, North Carolina, with the city-street exteriors shot in Chicago. For the wide shots of the twinkling city, an extraordinary 1:24 scale model of Manhattan's skyline was constructed, big enough for the directors to literally walk through like gods or giants. Designed by Dennis Gassner, the sets didn't resemble real places as much as grand, cinematic exaggerations

of real places. The effect is so heightened it borders on science fiction, and yet the film is intent on being a Capraesque parable. The steampunk, a Rube Goldberg machine of Terry Gilliam's *Brazil*, is found in the Hudsucker Building's infernal post room, where Norville begins his all-too-rapid rise to the top. Reticulating into a vast distance and including 35,000 fake letters, this crackpot shop floor is governed by a litany of unobservable rules: 'If you don't stamp it, they dock ya!!' Here too is the soul-crushing machinery of Chaplin's *Modern Times*, the angry sprawl of *Metropolis*, and a touch of Kafka's bureaucratic nightmares.

As deliberately as the film's clockwork is revealed (in one terrific joke, literally as clockwork!), it remains a surreal wonderland unlike anything the Coens have ever done. And as Norville and Amy's story struggles to gain any emotional ground, there are isolated moments of pure charm. Not least the sublime vignette where outside forces intervene in Norville's otherwise predestined life. Every inch a marvel of Coen visual dexterity and

Below: Charles Durning in
*The Hudsucker Proxy* (1994).

Opposite page: Tim Robbins,
Paul Newman and Jennifer Jason Leigh
in *The Hudsucker Proxy* (1994).

use of montage, we follow the rise of Norville's hula hoop from abject failure to national sensation. Referencing Albert Lamorisse's *The Red Balloon* (1956), a scarlet hoop escapes its allotted fate in the dumpster and rolls to the feet of a tiny boy, who begins the hula-hooping craze on the spot. The sight of the gawping faces of freckly children mesmerized by his spinning motion is magical.

If you accept it as pastiche, the film is a bountiful exercise in high style and rococo detail: the whirling board advertising new jobs; the shadow of the clock's second hand sweeping across Mussburger's office; Peter Gallagher's silky-smooth cameo as a lounge crooner. But the film was slammed for being an exercise in vain trickery with no larger social purpose, demeaning the worldliness of the directors it supposedly honoured. It pulled in too many different directions: farce, satire, allegory, homage and self-reflexive, technocratic grandeur. The ingredients of 1930s comedy don't fit the '50s. They had received harsh reviews before but not quite to this extent. Few critics took their side at all and box-office returns were less than $3 million in the US (although it did break even abroad). The Coens were crestfallen, but undeterred. They had tried to expand their canvas without compromising their vision, but big wasn't really their thing.

Paul Newman and Tim Robbins in *The Hudsucker Proxy* (1994).

# The unlikeliest heroes
## From *Fargo* to *O'Brother, Where Art Thou?*

Jeff Bridges in
*The Big Lebowski* (1998).

## This is a true story

*The Hudsucker Proxy* could easily have wrecked the career of a mainstream director. The indomitable brothers treated its failure with a mystified shrug and got on with their next project. Even before shooting had begun on the extravagant Tim Robbins comedy, they had been finishing two other scripts. Wisely, in hindsight, both required more conservative budgets. The more complete of these went by the intriguing title of *The Big Lebowski*. Inspired by their second stint in Los Angeles while filming *Barton Fink*, this was to be another distortion of film noir, although set in the early 1990s among the pot-pourri of subcultures that muster at the city's fringes. Chief among these Angeleno nobodies was an ageing stoner going by the nomenclature of The Dude, who only Jeff Bridges could usefully embody. Bridges, however, was tied up shooting Walter Hill's western *Wild Bill* (1995).

Thus, the Coens turned to the other script, featuring a character they had written with only one actress in mind — Joel's wife, Frances McDormand. With piquant brevity, it was called *Fargo* (1996), named after a town in Minnesota close to where the Coens grew up. Whimsically, Fargo would appear only once in the film (where Jerry first hires his kidnappers), the majority of events taking place in nearby Brainerd. The directors simply liked the way the word 'Fargo' sounded more suggestive. Of what, they had no idea. Eschewing the studio route (Warner politely vetoed the script), it would cost $6.5 million — not much more than the budget for *Raising Arizona*.

As the Faulkner-like W. P. Mayhew observes in *Barton Fink*, 'Truth is a tart that does not bear scrutiny.' It is certainly a relative concept for the Coens. They duck and weave their way through interviews, if not exactly lying, displaying a versatility with truth. Even Roderick Jaynes, the brothers' long-standing editor, turned out to be phantom, a cover story for the fact the brothers were their own editors. Across their films, characters are not who they claim to be, truths go unheeded, and even the firm ground of setting slips and slides into dream and fable.

Nothing is to be trusted in the Coen universe. *Fargo* opens with a lie. After the film became an unexpected hit, it emerged the title card's claim ('This is a true story…') wasn't the case at all. The ensuing tale of botched kidnapping was entirely made up. Yet, this being Coenesque, there *is* a kernel of truth to *Fargo* — a real-life story about an

William H. Macy in *Fargo* (1996).

exasperated Connecticut airline pilot who fed his nagging wife into a wood chipper. Exactly the kind of absurdly overcomplicated human evil that suggests Coen films are more like life than we care to admit. As their other films are blends of pop culture, their latest thriller was salted with reality. Moreover, suggesting however loosely that their film was based on truth had an ulterior motive in setting a naturalistic tone. Rather than sealed within the bounds of their proxy America, *Fargo* was to be the first Coen film to be located in the real world. Potentially, even an autobiographical place. But no one was suggesting its menagerie of psychos, rats, half-wits and big mouths was in any way representative of the real Minnesota.

## No line on the horizon

The look of *Fargo* was to match the grim white-out landscapes of the Minnesotan winters the Coens knew well. That sinister moment where you cannot tell with any certainty where the snow-covered ground stops and the blizzard-filled skies begin. There would be no horizon. A *tabula rasa* against which small-time misanthropy would freeze into murder. Deliberately veering away from the stifling artifice of *The Hudsucker Proxy*, the Coens attempted a documentary-like stateliness. Roger Deakins would shoot scenes with a single, static camera, but maintain an aura of strange beauty: the disappearance of red tail lights into nothingness, the figure of eight made by a car's tracks in the fresh snow of an open-air car park, the fairytale essence of the cabin in the woods. We can virtually feel the cold, but the filmmakers had to chase it around the Midwest. With bad fortune, the shoot coincided with the region's second warmest winter for a hundred years. Production shifted to northern Minnesota, North Dakota, Canada, and Fargo's one appearance had to be faked. The story wasn't to be architecturally pleasing either. Unthinkably,

Frances McDormand in *Fargo* (1996).

Following pages: Peter Stormare and Steve Buscemi in *Fargo* (1996).

the heroine doesn't make her entrance for thirty-three minutes. The rulebook is buried in the snow; there are no cues about how we are supposed to react. Laugh or cry?

The plot evolves from wretched car salesman Jerry Lundegaard's plan to hire a pair of thugs to fake the kidnap of his wife, forcing her wealthy father to pay the ransom and unknowingly settle Jerry's financial woes. Why these two particular crooks and how he has run up the debt are never mentioned. They don't figure. The point is the banality of the crime and its perpetrators. Especially Jerry: this wheedling milquetoast utterly out of his depth, unravelling in a virtuoso display of jabbering high anxiety by William H. Macy. The kidnappers in question, Carl Showalter and Gaear Grimsrud, were written for the duo of Steve Buscemi and Peter Stormare. Buscemi rattles on at such a fever pitch in *Fargo*, the Coens saw fit to shoot him in the jaw. But Carl is more reasonable than

we might think. However immoral his actions, he is trying (and failing) to maintain a grip on sanity. Something that can't be said for Gaear. Why they are partners, and they seem to have only recently met, is another of the film's ambiguities. It just wracks up the tension. As their relationship inevitably disintegrates, the bodies of innocent bystanders will be left facedown in the snow, and a fake kidnap will become a real one.

Frances McDormand, who deservingly won an Oscar for this unflappable good-heart pregnant policewoman, catches the perfect frequency: winningly humorous but never patronizing, springing the film into an unforeseen dimension. She was actually written as an extension of the insane world of *Fargo*, and Ethan always thought of her as annoying. Both brothers and McDormand were stunned at how the audience took to her. Buscemi was supposed to be our cipher, the outsider in this land of crazies. What they hadn't noticed was that 41

Marge's simple goodness, completely new to a Coen film, presents their disenchanted view of America with a laurel of hope. Jerry represents the odious striving of the American Dream, whereas Marge is liberated from its grip, and thus content. She is free of accepted cinematic practice: a heroine who is unaffected, plain speaking, and successful in a man's role. But it is the women in Coen films who understand and uphold the rules, and safeguard the ethics. As with *Raising Arizona*, McDormand, and the film, came under fire for their depiction of Minnesotans as simple-minded bumpkins wrapped in puffer jackets. But McDormand couldn't have worked harder to finesse Marge's persona (the 'Minnesota Nice'), using local voice coaches to perfect the stoic ease of a people for whom sub-zero is mild. And Joel jeered that if people wanted to be offended, they would be.

The Coens deliberately walk a fine line between comedy and parody, rarely setting out to judge or mock, but drawn by nature towards distinct flavours of ethnic groups and fillips of odd behaviour (as well as deliberately using stereotypes). It is what makes their characters so interesting. Yes, it can feel pointed, but we shouldn't neglect the degree of self-portrait on show. They explore their own place as non-conformist Americans (i.e. not the Americans of Hollywood movies) and they always feel a connection with the places they depict. In *Fargo* it was a location they knew by heart: the taciturn, emotional-sidestepping world where they had grown up. Autobiography is too strong a word, but in tapping a more personal vein (many of the characters' names are those of old friends and colleagues) they finally connected with a wider audience.

Taking $60 million worldwide, *Fargo* became their biggest hit to date and the reviews were ecstatic. They were invited to the Oscars, to win Best Original Screenplay and Best Actress out of seven nominations. The film itself remains for many the high-water mark of Coenesque. The brothers' pessimism offset by a gentle morality that feels genuinely meant rather than booby-trapped with irony. Marge, settling back beneath the quilt of her quiet, fastidious home life, sighs at the wickedness she has witnessed, the strange cruelty of the world that is quite beyond her. She maybe a funny-walking, funny-talking yokel, but she is never a fool and never a cliché.

## Chandleresque

Fans of the Coens' seventh film are often surprised to learn that it performed poorly at the box office, having run the gamut of critical reception on its release in the spring of 1998. While many lauded its weird charm, engaging characters and abstract take on noir, *The Big Lebowski* wasn't *Fargo*. More concerned critics scolded what they saw as a return to bad habits. When the film debuted at the Sundance Film Festival in snowy Utah, critics walked out, somehow offended. Perhaps it is the 292 expletives, a new record for the regularly profane Coens. It would make only $27 million worldwide, and looked set to be confined to the dustbin of Coen experimentation. History, however, would think differently; history, it transpires, likes to bowl.

Such now is *The Big Lebowski*'s place as the most adored of Coen films, it has become more than

a Coen film. There are currently eleven Lebowski Fests, where bearded devotees of the film's supposed ethos gather at bowling alleys across America to quote lines, drink White Russians (The Dude's tipple of choice) and bowl. The film has taken a transcendent place in popular culture: from T-shirts to academic studies debating such issues as 'Lebowski/ Mnemosyne: Cultural Memory, Cultural Authority, and Forgetfulness'.

If the brothers had made their James M. Cain film (in *Blood Simple*), their Dashiell Hammett film (in *Miller's Crossing*), then *The Big Lebowski* was to be their variant on Raymond Chandler. Even more so than their previous adventures in noir, it was given an absurdist slant. They would replace the central, hard-bitten gumshoe with the most unlikely figure they could conceive in the maze of a bewildering Chandleresque plot. As he was also to conceivably be a denizen of the wider circle of Los Angeles, the answer was an ageing pothead known as The Dude, even though, significantly as it would prove, his real name is Jeffrey Lebowski. In other words, they were attempting a Zen thriller. Both through the Coens' writing and Bridges' magnanimous performance, The Dude would take on unforeseen dimensions: this relic of the 1960s, a Rip Van Winkle who has slept for decades, waking in the 1990s to set aside radicalism for comfort. What touches people is that he is a becalmed soul, interested only in maintaining an acceptable status quo. He will be thrust far beyond his comfort zone by a set of bamboozling events triggered by a case of mistaken identity (with the paraplegic millionaire Jeffrey Lebowski, played by David Huddleston) and the theft of his precious, ratty-ass rug. We are told so many times that it 'really tied the room together', it becomes the film's mantra. In main, the plot encircles the kidnap of his namesake's nymphomaniac trophy wife, but includes an avant-garde artist, a devious pornographer, a former German electronica band and the rapid erosion of The Dude's steady if unproductive lifestyle, as symbolized by the gradual destruction of his comfortably battered 1973 Ford Torino. Many factions will assail The Dude, but the biggest thorn in his side is his best friend and bowling partner Walter Sobchak (another fulminating sidekick drafted for the charismatic volume of John Goodman). Walter in his way embodies the film's manic eclecticism: a Polish–American Vietnam vet who has converted to Judaism, and demonstrates a flux of unlikely intellectualism, with his own cornucopia of quotations from Shakespeare to Talmudic lore, and psychotic fury. His actions might be dubious, but his courage and devotion to The Dude are unquestionable.

Walter also pinpoints one of the film's central themes: misrepresentation. People and things are not what they appear or are taken for – we need to look deeper. From The Dude being the wrong 'Lebowski' and the kidnap not being a kidnap, a terrier is taken for a Pomeranian, a ferret for a marmot, we meet a Jew who is not a Jew, an arrogant Hispanic bowler who used to be a pederast, and a cowboy narrates the story. A world of deception populated by an array of Coen regulars and debutants, among them Peter Stormare, John Turturro, Steve Buscemi, Julianne Moore and Philip Seymour Hoffman, ricochet off one another in Brownian motion. The film is full of phoneys, yet feels genuine, which is because, in the case of Walter and The Dude, they were shaped from real people, eccentric Angelenos the Coens got to know on their travels to the city. Film producer Peter Exline was a touchy Vietnam veteran who liked to tell everyone his rug 'really tied the room together'. He also tells the story of having his car stolen, and how his best friend, big Lew Abernathy, a Vietnam vet turned private

Opposite page: Jeff Bridges in *The Big Lebowski* (1998).

Right: John Turturro in *The Big Lebowski* (1998).

Following pages: Jeff Bridges and John Goodman in *The Big Lebowski* (1998).

eye, traced the culprit via a piece of homework they
found on the back seat. Walter bears the hallmarks
of bulky film director John Milius, who had written
*Apocalypse Now* and directed *Big Wednesday* (note the
'Big'), an elegiac hymn to California's surfing (rather
than bowling) culture, set against the backdrop of
the Vietnam War. Jeff Dowd, a regular attendee of
Lebowski Fests, is obviously the basis for The Dude
given he is known as 'The Dude'. This former pot-
smoking radical was a member of the Seattle Seven,
an anti-Vietnam protest group, just as his fictional
counterpart confesses to have been. Joel noted that
more elements of *The Big Lebowski* were true than
in *Fargo*.

### The Valley of the shadow of death

From the very play of the title (*The Big Sleep*/*The
Big Lebowski*), it is clear this is a comic refraction
of Chandler's noir through a shape-shifting but
urbane early 1990s. The Coens claimed the only

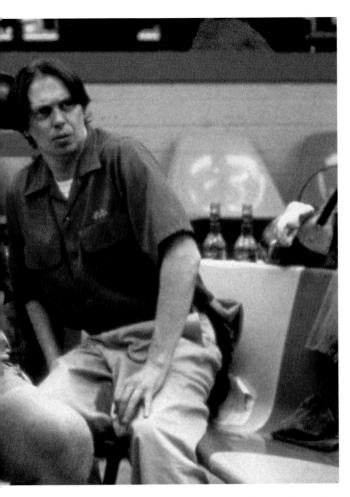

reason they chose this era was to give Walter a foreign war to bitch about (Saddam Hussein hands out bowling shoes in The Dude's dream while the Gulf War tries vainly to be noticed on TV sets). There's something about American insularity that needles the brothers, how distant wars gain mythical status in America's sleepy armchairs. Otherwise, like The Dude, the plot slips the borders of its own time. But rather than an antecedent of Hawksian camp, the Coens are co-opting his approach and turning it to their own ends. Significantly, the brothers' primary film reference was not Hawks's classic (*The Big Sleep*, 1946), but Robert Altman's 1973 reinterpretation of Chandler, *The Long Goodbye*. Akin to *The Big Lebowski*, Altman replaces the hard-boiled Philip Marlowe with Elliot Gould's nitwit Marlowe. Both The Dude and Gould's Marlowe have no capacity for their role as entrepreneurial investigators, fumbling but likeable humans adrift in the currents of crime. Both plots make an archetype of incomprehensibility. As

is so often the case in Coenesque, this is a consequence of the characters rewriting their own part of the story. Walter, especially, happily readjusts reality to fit his viewpoint. From the point of trying to fake the ransom drop (unbeknown to them, a fake ransom) Walter and The Dude bring catastrophe upon themselves.

Visually the film maintains *Fargo*'s shift to naturalism, the Coens shooting on location in the sprawl of the Valley, sleepy Venice and surreal Malibu (where Ben Gazzara's 'tasteful' pornographer Jackie Treehorn holds court in a bubble of 1970s sleaze). There is a glazed, smoggy light by day and a smoky orange glow to the night. Yet there is no uniform design, rather a hybrid of styles. Uniquely among Coen films, this isn't a Los Angeles of the mind rather than the city's true nature. A landscape equal to the Coens' imagination forestalls their instinctive drift into the mythological. It is *already* the Dream Factory, although touchstones of *The Big Sleep* do emerge out of the outré fug: the Lebowski mansion with its roaring fires and titanic desks represents the Sternwood mansion, while Bunny the nympho wife stands in for Sternwood's wayward daughter Carmen. Los Angeles grants the film a wonderful double life: altered state and Chandler's mean streets.

*The Big Lebowski* presents a dizzying barrage of characters, plots, locations, language, themes and devices; even the soundtrack is a mixtape of cover versions of Dude-centric oddities. If anything, we are in a pastiche of Coenesque itself that delights in clashing generic concepts together to create something new. For Ethan the mix was 'emblematic' of the chaos of Los Angeles. It embodies the city's melange of cultures, styles, crimes and ethics, how it acts as a microcosm of America, collecting the waifs and strays of America — the fallen artists, war veterans, dropouts and sleazebags, the sprawling, ratty-ass metropolis that really ties the nation together. And The Dude will travel through this city of the night on his Chandleresque journey towards … Well, towards himself. His character arc returns him to square one.

## The noble laughter of the common man

There is something curiously old-fashioned about the Coens. They have a traditionalist persuasion. Take, for example, the antiquated syntax they feed 49 their characters, this love of squeezing a musicality out of unusual words like 'paterfamilias', 'malfeasance' or 'unguent'. Drag a word out of them, and they too speak in a scrupulous fashion, constructing sentences as if laying each word down on parchment. The Coens have often talked of the 'exoticism' the past offers, how they naturally gravitate backwards in time. However, once relocated in the past they are rarely concerned with veracity, or a fixed period at all. Striking a familiar chord, Holly Hunter, about to return to the fold for the first time since *Raising Arizona*, claimed their films were set in a 'realm of their mind'. [10] Just take the case in point,

*O Brother, Where Art Thou?* (2000): a prisoners-on-the-lam, comic picaresque set in a romanticized, if not mythologized, Depression-era Mississippi, based on a subplot from a Preston Sturges film and Homer's *The Odyssey* (which the Coens claim never to have read); a gumbo they may have cribbed from *A Dozen Tough Jobs*, a 1989 novella by Howard Waldrop that recounts the Labours of Hercules in Mississippi. The Coens call it their hayseed epic.

Let's start with the Sturges part of the equation. In Sturges's 1941 escapade *Sullivan's Travels*, an idealistic Hollywood director called Sullivan, played by Joel McCrea, disguising himself as a hobo, goes

John Turturro, Tim Blake Nelson and George Clooney in *O'Brother* (2000).

in search of the common man, intending to make an important film that will encompass his hopes, his dreams and his embattled pride — that whole *Barton Fink* feeling. He will call this great work of art, *O Brother, Where Art Thou?* What he discovers on his travels, apart from Veronica Lake, is that what the common man likes is to escape his burdens by falling about laughing to cartoons. Thus, Sullivan gives up on his precious film. That's fundamentally the point of *Sullivan's Travels* as a whole: its grandiosity is a joke; it just wants to make us laugh. The Coens also profess that there is nothing more noble than eliciting merriment. So, with tongues

lodged firmly in cheeks, they decided to make the film-within-a film that Sullivan never does, a film where all the Steinbeckian backwoods grandeur of its Southern locations is equally a joke. Even sillier, it was to bear the Olympian imprimatur of *The Odyssey* (which we'll come to shortly). Their 'common man' would come in the guise of three dolts recently absconded from a chain gang (a further lift from *Sullivan's Travels*) who bumble across Mississippi seeking buried treasure, although the only member of the trio with any idea of its whereabouts is the majestically unreliable Ulysses Everett McGill (George Clooney). In his tow come the feebleminded

# The musical tradition of *O Brother, Where Art Thou?*

When the Coen brothers mined the tradition of bluegrass, country and blues music to serve as a backdrop for their comic picaresque *O Brother, Where Art Thou?* (2000) they could never have imagined they were starting a revival of a whole genre of music. Using the talents of musician and music historian T-Bone Burnett as curator (he had also worked on *The Big Lebowski*), the film's musical line-up included Ralph Stanley, Norman Blake, Alison Krauss, Emmylou Harris, Gillian Welch, The Cox Family and The Whites: a who's who of country and blues stars. They also dusted down some original recordings to lend proceedings a bit of smoky gravity. Some of the soundtracks' impressive stars even turn up in the film: Welch takes the briefest cameo as a shopper in search of the sold-out Soggy Bottom Boys hit, while The Fairfield Four play the crooning grave-diggers at the very end. Any songs peformed 'within' the film were usually synced to play-back, but Tim Blake Nelson, who has a lovely voice, sang live on set. The soundtrack would go on to become a stand-alone success, selling more than seven million copies and winning five Grammys.

The music of *O Brother, Where Art Thou?* amounts to a genuine 'folk' music born in the 1920s and '30s in the mountains and the delta regions of the Southern states, as well as on the chain gangs. The Coens were showing a cultural awareness beyond their usual literary and cinematic cornerstones. They even decided to expand these musical horizons beyond the context of the film itself, holding a benefit concert at the Ryman Auditorium in Nashville and hiring renowned documentary maker D. A. Pennebaker (who directed the Bob Dylan doc *Don't Look Back*) to make a concert film of the occasion. Released as *Down from the Mountain* (executive-produced by the Coens), it was heralded by critics as a triumphant film about America itself as seen through this, as Burnett puts it, 'profound sound'.

Tim Blake Nelson, John Turturro and George Clooney in *O'Brother* (2000).

Tim Blake Nelson, George Clooney
and John Turturro in *O'Brother* (2000).

brace of touchy Pete (John Turturro) and mild-man-nered Delmar (Tim Blake Nelson). They will encounter every manner of real, classical and diabolic trials before reaching a form of redemption as bluegrass troubadours The Soggy Bottom Boys.

*O Brother, Where Art Thou?* is the most benign of Coen films, light on violence, a family movie from an odd sort of angle. Joel amused himself (and his brother), branding the script a Three Stooges movie with Homeric overtones. Everett marks the apotheosis of Coen windbags. Clooney was such a natural choice for Everett, the Coens didn't enquire elsewhere. He has that mix of A-list looks and a willingness to make fun of them. Thankfully, it turned out Clooney was a Coen-obsessive. 'I can't think of one [film] I didn't love,' he enthused, [11] and agreed without seeing the script. Working together would cement a mutual admiration, and Clooney would become an important member the Coen family.

While the actors are forever slaves to the script, the meticulous detail in Coen characters in the hands of meticulously chosen actors divulges humanity. Even in the midst of legendary trials, born two thousand years earlier, Everett won't settle until he dons the correct brand of pomade. 'I don't want FOP damn it, I'm a Dapper Dan man!' bellows Clooney at a bemused retailer. Dapper Dan is one of those exquisite grace notes of Coen design, characterizing not only their leading man's

pernickety levels of vanity and lending a tang of period authenticity, but providing the scent by which the authorities trace their quarry. Felled by the signature of your own hair gel.

## A Greek sailor's better-known encounters
The film's Homeric strand figures as a blatant parody of the epic style, to chime with the ruined classicism of the South in which the film is set. Roger Deakins excels himself in draining colour from the frames, giving the film the 'hand-tinted' sepia hue of period daguerreotypes (this was the first film to be digitally colour-corrected in its entirety). However, shooting in the 120-degree heat around Canton, Mississippi, provided a sun-slaked aridity to help them on their way to the required dusty Delta, Eudora Welty look. Where art *The Odyssey*? Beyond Everett's extended cognomen, we are tasked with spotting the artful insertion of the Greek sailor's better-known encounters. Lee Weaver turns sightless seer Tiresias into a blind railwayman toiling his handcart down the tracks; the '*syreens*' seduce the boys with their song while washing their clothes in the river; the Lotus Eaters become a congregation going trancelike to their baptism; Hunter's Penny is clearly Penelope; and John Goodman makes a lively Cyclops. In Coen films God's workers make for untrustworthy men. Religion is both an outrageous scam and a vehicle for salvation. Another

Holly Hunter in *O'Brother* (2000).

of the many storytelling seductions that jostle for attention in *O Brother, Where Art Thou?* include homespun wisdom, old wives' tales, philosophies, scientific reasoning, sales pitches, the emergent hubbub of advertising hoardings and electioneering speak, plus, not to be forgotten, music. No one was immune to the parallels between the oral traditions of the soundtrack's blues, gospel and bluegrass songs and that of Homer himself.

*O Brother, Where Art Thou?* brought in decent reviews (admiration for its quick wit, playfulness and Clooney's delightful self-parody), and a good return at the box office (its budget was $26 million and it made $71 million worldwide). But there was the nagging sensation that the film had nothing to say beyond its mild satire of America's upbringing. Yet, amid the comic gusto, at times reaching the *Looney Tunes* pitch of *Raising Arizona*, the film achieves poignancy. Supine around a campfire, the

three heroes pledge what they will do with their share of the treasure. Delmar, who appears touched by an angelic innocence (Everett presses us to see him as a 'paradigm of hope'), bears notice of the crushing effects of the Depression: 'You ain't no kind of man if you ain't got land.' We feel another ripple of Coen concern over the soulless monopolies of big business. And men trying to be more than they are.

# The Coens' favourite filmmaker

Arguably the strongest cinematic inspiration for the Coens, the screwball flourishes of Preston Sturges are deeply embedded in the Coen aesthetic. The brothers directly reference Sturges in the elaborate comic workings of *The Hudsucker Proxy*, their spangled contraption made from 1930s Hollywood tropes, and the title of *O Brother, Where Art Thou?* references the film-within-a-film that goes unmade in Sturges's Hollywood satire *Sullivan's Travels*. To varying degrees, Sturges's experiments with narrative form and genre, as well as his satirical edge, whip-crack dialogue and deep-seated morality can be detected in every single Coen film.

Sturges's own life also has the ring of Coen eccentricity.

Born in Chicago, his wealthy and domineering mother Mary Desti was friends with Isadora Duncan and had an affair with occultist Aleister Crowley. Sturges was to take the long way round to Hollywood, trying out stockbroking, the Air Force and running his mother's fashion firm Maison Desti. Ousted by his beloved mater, he turned to inventing, including kiss-proof lipstick and a ticker-tape machine. While in New York, Sturges chanced acting on Broadway and then, with more success, playwriting, hitting it big with *Strictly Dishonorable*, which ran for sixteen months and landed him a contract with Paramount. Despite earning a princely $2,500 a week, Sturges became increasingly frustrated with the formulaic uses to which directors put his words and yearned for creative control. So he offered Paramount the script for *The Great McGinty* for a dollar if they allowed him to direct. The deal eventually closed at $10 with Sturges the director, only to confound his masters at every turn. Akin to what the Coens hold dear, Sturges wrote with a keen ear for the variances of American vernacular, planted his films well away from the Hollywood patch and developed a stock company of regular actors featuring Joel McCrea, George Anderson and Eddie Bracken. Marking a creative high, the key Sturges films came in a row: *The Great McGinty* (1940; a hobo ends up running for office), *Sullivan's Travels* (1941; a disillusioned director goes in search of the common man), *The Lady Eve* (1941; a tricky romance forms between a rich heir and a con-woman), *The Palm Beach Story* (1942; an estranged New York couple hotfoot it to Florida) and *Hail The Conquering Hero* (1944; a small town's attempts to turn a returning Marine into a mayor, even though his hay fever kept him from seeing combat). Sturges was married four times, and died of a heart attack at the Algonquin Hotel, Manhattan, in 1959.

Veronica Lake and Joel McCrea in *Sullivan's Travels* by Preston Sturges (1941).

# The strangest villains

From *The Man Who Wasn't There* to *The Ladykillers*

Ethan Coen and Marlon
Wayans on the set
of *The Ladykillers* (2004).

## Appearances can be deceptive

Shot in an exquisite, velvety black and white, *The Man Who Wasn't There* (2001) appears to be without irony. Here is a crystalline noir set in the luminous California of *Double Indemnity* (1944) and *Kiss Me Deadly* (1955). Had the Coens finally set aside their games to play it straight? (As straight as noir ever gets.) Not quite. The idea of shooting in black and white had been on their minds since *The Hudsucker Proxy*, another hint of their appreciation for old Hollywood, and beneath the handsome veneer the new film remained pure Coenesque. Only the irony refuses to be hurried. Returning to California, but not Los Angeles, this was also a return to the sour cosmos of their venerated crime writers. As with *Blood Simple*, the focus was once more on the homespun deviance of James M. Cain. The plot works almost as an inverse of his *Mildred Pierce* (1941), a book the brothers have considered adapting, but the story of Ed Crane first glimmered into life when the Coens unearthed a poster featuring a assortment of '40s-style haircuts while researching *The Hudsucker Proxy*, and was written under the working title of 'The Barber Project'.

As the Coens liked to explain, as vaporously as the ever-present cigarette smoke, the story was set in 1949, and involved a small-town barber who wanted to get into dry cleaning. The telling distinction is that their leading man, played by Billy Bob Thornton, barely utters a word within the film. 'Me, I don't talk much', Crane informs us in the somnolent voice-over. That's just it — we will constantly hear his account of events from some obscure place, possibly the grave. There is a ghostly quality, as if Ed is haunting his own story. His voice as sterile as the cleaning process he pursues, Ed will report on the increasingly bizarre circumstances that begin with a man in a toupee asking him for a haircut. What's funnier than a man with fake hair asking for a trim? But Ed isn't funny. Not a clown like The Dude. In fact, *The Man Who Wasn't There* is like a photographic negative of *The Big Lebowski*, where everything is damped down and seeped of colour. Ed's isn't a voice-over in the heehaw timbre of Hi from *Raising Arizona* or The Stranger in *The Big Lebowski*, but a persistent, analytical discourse that allows entry into his head. A soundtrack to his atomically decaying half-life. This remarkable, quasi-novelistic approach steeps everything in his colourless psyche. Black and white isn't just about style or movie history, it is narrative: Ed sees the world in monochrome.

Roger Deakins shot in colour and converted to black and white for the added lustre and contrast.

Frances McDormand and Billy Bob Thornton in *The Man Who Wasn't There* (2001).

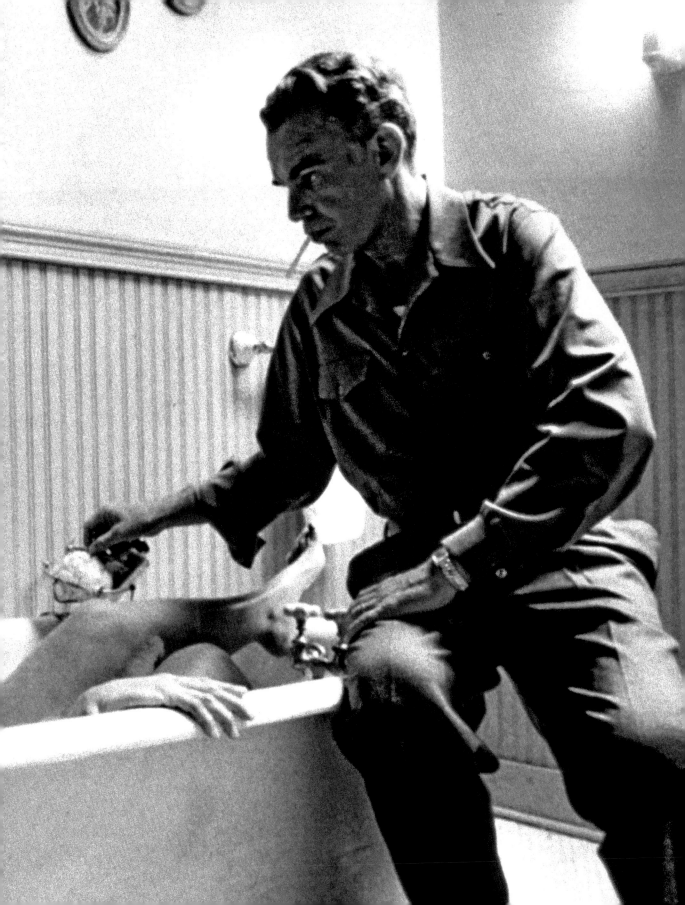

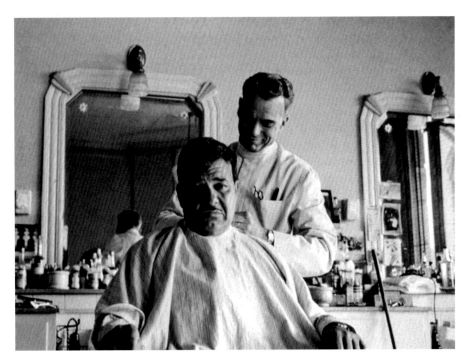

Thus the film doesn't feel like a copy of a 1940s or '50s noir, but a fellow traveller. There is emotional texture in the way light catches the eyes, and a foreboding written into the shadows that swim across faces and walls, something simultaneously creepy and absorbing in the camera's funereal pace. This doesn't come cheap — the film cost $20 million, mustered independently from a faithful set of partners: Gramercy, Working Title, and Ted Hope and James Shamus at Good Machine, key figures (who would later form Focus Features) in promoting ambitious material at the fringes of the studio system. In the recesses of Ed's dormant imagination, there are strange awakenings. He harkens to the call of the American Dream, to be a better man, but it brings with it disturbing visions of UFOs, paranoia and murder.

### What kind of man are you?

Billy Bob Thornton had come to know the Coens at the typically unctuous film-industry functions none of them relished attending. They had talked about working together at some unfixed point. Thornton thought it no more than politeness. But the offer came — this film about a barber induced to first blackmail and then murder his wife's lover. Like Clooney before him, Thornton was content. 'The thing is,' the actor claimed with succinct wisdom, 'they just don't suck.' [12]

Their third Californian film is far removed from the assorted residents of *The Big Lebowski* or the shadowy Hollywood of *Barton Fink*. Here is a provincial community like in *Fargo* or *Blood Simple*, another 'ordinary' place in which crime can fester. The film is set and was partially shot in Santa Rosa, where Hitchcock made *Shadow of a Doubt* (1943), alongside *Psycho* (1960), Joel's favourite of his thrillers. *Shadow of a Doubt* brings evil to a quiet community: Joseph Cotten plays the psycho with a smile and there is something of his look if not his grin in Ed. In truth, there doesn't really seem to be a villain at all in *The Man Who Wasn't There*. Yes, Doris (a beautifully modulated Frances McDormand), Ed's faithless, striving wife, is having an affair with her boss, the brutish hard-to-love department store manager Big Dave Brewster (James Gandolfini). But in many respects they are the victims: one murdered, the other wrongly incriminated for the murder. Ed, by chance, is the perpetrator, but nothing about him is exactly evil. Nothing about him suggests anything more than an eerie longing. His actions could almost be in slow motion. What kind of man is that?

### Alien nation

The DVD edition of *The Man Who Wasn't There* features the only commentary the directors have yet given. They chat alongside Thornton, and between the inevitable guffaws and awkward pauses, give a good account of the film. Actor and directors point out the increasing degrees of emotion Ed displays, as if thawed by his predicament. Is he entering the world? This arc is faint, but after Doris is incriminated, we see glimmers of hurt, a fractional increase in dialogue. What are we to make of his dreams? When unconscious Ed sees apparitions of UFOs scouring the earth with a bright, white light, production designer Dennis Gassner repeats the motif in light fittings and hubcaps. The directors ended up dropping a scene where tiny alien 'ant men' sneak in beneath Ed's door, which Joel described as their 'Kafka break'. The film's style joins noir to the chiaroscuro of 1950s B movies like *Invasion of the Body Snatchers*, whose star Kevin McCarthy was another touchstone for the look of Ed. Are we witnessing the dissolution of Ed's psyche? Perhaps he was mad all along. Ed is so internalized ('Ed' equals 'head'?), he has become alien to the world. Or is it the world that is alien? Between pivotal events skulks the paranoia that pervaded post-war America, that fear of a changing world, of threats from outside — communism, atomic bombs or alien invaders — while the real danger lurked within the living rooms and barbershops.

Such a strange offering was unlikely to be broadly commerical, and the film's remoteness was never bridged, leaving it to peter out at takings of $18.9 million worldwide. Like its enigmatic leading character, it has been somewhat forgotten, unfairly viewed as a lesser light in the Coen canon. The reviews lauded its luscious style, the more subdued play on movie tropes and Thornton's wonderfully restrained performance. Some critics wondered if the Coens had been inspired by Albert Camus' existential novel *The Stranger* (1942), whose first person dialogue is echoed in Ed's nascent philosophizing. [13]

To expand on his defence of Doris Crane, self-aggrandizing lawyer Freddy Reidenschneider (a jabbering Tony Shalhoub, the anti-Ed) calls upon Heisenberg's Uncertainty Principle. At heart, as he reads it, the universe is unknowable. To try and make sense of the world, and by association make sense of the Coens, makes fools and murderers of us all. Call it the Coen Uncertainty Principle.

**Vanity unfair**

With *Fargo*'s success, for all its plaudits, dwindling into the past, the Coens were in need of a hit. While there were scripts in the vault, nothing seemed to readily suggest itself. The studios were pacing like expectant fathers, hoping the brothers might be nursing the next *Fargo* rather than, say, something black and white or obscurely Finkish. In the spring of 2001 it sounded like Universal had got what it wanted: the prospective tale of a ruthless divorce lawyer who falls in love with a gold-digging *femme*

*fatale* — the kind of romantic farce that might have jostled for space on a studio roster in the 1930s. And yet, this was a rare foray into a contemporary setting in the mock-opulent mansions and glass-partitioned offices that play host to Los Angeles's stratospherically wealthy, a glazed suburb to the movie industry. It came thick with barbs directed towards the conveyor-belt marriages of the rich and famous. The prevailing joke is we can't be sure where the avarice and manipulation stop and romance begins. If less death than usual, not counting an unsuccessful, asthmatic hitman named Wheezy Joe, there would still be plenty of wickedness. It sounded, well, rather straightforward for the Coens. Maybe because it wasn't their idea.

The storyline originated at Universal in the early 1990s, a typically many-fathered pitch credited to Robert Ramsey, Matthew Stone and John Romano. The studio had hired the Coens solely as writers in 1993 to pep it up with their caustic wit. They had no intention of directing. It was too commercial for their tastes. The brothers delivered a pop cocktail of social satire and romantic farce, in which the growing affection between husband-devouring Marylin Rexroth and unbeatable divorce attorney Miles Massey might be an elaborate con. The script drifted around Hollywood for eight years before the Coen brothers were finally persuaded to direct it.

Despite Clooney's ever-willing currents of self-parody, *Intolerable Cruelty* (2003) never feels wholly a Coen creation. Something is lacking. At $60 million it was a huge step up in budget. And as for a screwball battle of the sexes? Crucially, there is a no great chemistry, romantic or comic, between Clooney and Catherine Zeta-Jones, whose delivery is too sluggish and whispery to recall the peppy attack of Katharine Hepburn. We are not meant to entirely trust Marylin's motives. She is a rare ethically suspect Coen female, but remains very much in control. The Coens fail to find much within Zeta-Jones — neither resonance with the past nor a deconstruction of the present. Not as immediately glamorous, but a Holly Hunter or a Frances McDormand would have more than matched Clooney's boyish

Catherine Zeta-Jones in *Intolerable Cruelty* (2003).

Opposite page: George Clooney in *Intolerable Cruelty* (2003).

# The double life of the Coens' editor

Perhaps we should have suspected something funny was going on given he never appeared to work for anyone else. More to the fact, no one else had even met him. But he bore credits on both *Blood Simple* and *Barton Fink*, and by *Fargo* (1996) Roderick Jaynes had landed a nomination for an Academy Award for his excellent editing. What we knew of him as a person could be drawn only from the published *Collected Screenplays 1*, to which Jaynes contributed a pontificating introduction, remarking on 'the Borstal sensibility of the boys' early efforts', and was allegedly an aged journeyman editor from Hove, Sussex, in England. Once home to the Coens' grandfather. Jaynes had apparently previously worked on a British comedy called *The Mad Weekend* (with Alastair Sim), *Beyond Mombassa* [sic] and *Operation Fort Petticoat* – none of which could be traced.

When the Academy tried to locate Jaynes, following his nomination, the jig was up. Having had their cheeky plan of dispatching to the Oscars Albert Finney in disguise as Jaynes prohibited by the Academy (all proxies had been nixed following Marlon Brando sending a Native American girl in his stead in 1973), the Coens had to come clean that their editor was actually a pseudonym for the two of them, and had only been dreamt up as they were rather embarrassed over the number of credits they were racking up. Although quizzed about his whereabouts on the night, they valiantly maintained, clearly enjoying extending the life of another ripe Coen character, that he was 'back at home in Haywards Heath watching cricket'. Furthermore, not actually existing has done little to halt his career – Roderick Jaynes has edited every Coen film since.

Catherine Zeta-Jones and George Clooney in *Intolerable Cruelty* (2003).

Opposite page: George Clooney and Catherine Zeta-Jones on the set of *Intolerable Cruelty* (2003).

folly. Still, Roger Deakins's visual palette revels in the literally superficial. The Coens have made a fetish of gleaming surfaces throughout their films (tables, floors, windscreens, even sunglasses), but here it becomes the signature aesthetic, from the marbled Beverly Hills parlours to the snow-bright glint of Miles's whitened teeth.

These people don't belong to a genre but, rather, an exaggerated perception of Californian vanity. However, the narcissism of the rich feels too soft a target for the cunning of Coenesque. Formally speaking, this is the only true Coen romance, but only sporadically does it catch light. The main courtroom sequence, in which Clooney's amoral Miles plies his legal magic on behalf of a philandering husband, gathers the vibrato pitch of stage farce. Rather than evoking cinema's vaunted history of legal drama, with their taste for low-culture the Coens are playing on the endless television re-runs

of lawyer shows they soaked up in their youth: *Perry Mason*, *Ironside* and *The Defenders*. They prove on stronger ground making sport of the legal drama, another realm of intractable rules and obscure procedures. Herb Myerson (Tom Aldredge), head of Miles's firm, is presented as an ancient, evil wizard, entombed behind his desk, sucking on an oxygen supply. And when Marylin and Miles duel with Shakespeare and Christopher Marlowe quotations, the back-and-forth between impenetrable legalese and romantic poetry provides some exhilarating contrasts. Bringing together the conniving female, the male dupe and the callous city, *Intolerable Cruelty* is perhaps another of the Coens' twists on noir.

## A tincture of British

Neither was a remake of the 1955 Ealing comedy something that had been gestating in the Coen minds. Neither Joel nor Ethan had seen the film

Tom Hanks, J. K. Simmons, Marlon Wayans, Tzi Ma and Ryan Hurst in *The Ladykillers* (2004).

since childhood, although there is a line in *Blood Simple* ('Who looks stupid now?' uttered by M. Emmet Walsh's corrupt private eye Loren Visser) that is a lift from the original film. So something must have struck a chord. Directed by Alexander Mackendrick, it is the tale of a mismatched gang of crooks, led by the ghastly Professor Marcus (Alec Guinness), who lay up at the King's Cross residence of a very little old lady (Katie Johnson) to plan their next robbery. She is fooled into thinking they are an amateur string quartet, thrilled a little culture has roamed her way. But as she becomes increasingly suspicious, the gang (which includes Peter Sellers, Herbert Lom and Cecil Parker) attempt to 'silence' their landlady, only to fall foul of fate themselves, their bodies dispatched to Hell on the steam trains that run behind her terraced London street.

British and genteel, Joel confessed, wasn't really their thing.[14] Another half-truth. Their father Ed is American only having been born in the USA; his father Victor Coen was British, a barrister in the Inns of Court in London. Having grown up in London, Ed Coen retained a British taste in movies, encouraging his sons to take in the Ealing comedies. This tincture of British in the Coen blood perhaps makes sense of the natural reserve, warding off of fame, gallows humour and matter-of-factness in speech. And maybe explains the lure of *The Ladykillers*. It proved a relatively swift writing assignment, taking only two months. Working in reverse to their normal orientation, they modernized William Rose's Oscar-nominated script, uprooting it from a sooty post-war London to present-day Pascagoula, Mississippi, lulling beneath the humid air, as languidly bland as Fargo is frozen solid.

It appears an interesting intersection of two distinct comic styles in *The Ladykillers* (2004): the Ealing and the Coen. Not entirely dissimilar, both enjoy twisting parochial stereotypes, but not entirely fitting together. As with *Intolerable Cruelty*, it never feels as if the Coens were wholeheartedly committed. Whatever the outcome, their films had been personal expressions. This was another square studio project being forced into a round Coen-hole.

### Pantomime villains

Another temptation for the Coens may have been the opportunity to crack open an A-list Hollywood

Marlon Wayans and J. K. Simmons in *The Ladykillers* (2004).

star as they had done with Jeff Bridges and George Clooney. Only when it had fallen to them to direct had they thought of Hanks as the pantomimic Professor Goldthwait Higginson Dorr III. In turn, Hanks only read the script because of its two authors, curious how it would prove 'Coenesque'. He, like Bridges and Clooney before him, was keen on both the credibility and freedom a Coen film offers. Like Woody Allen, they had become a badge of honour among mainstream actors, an emblem of an actor's versatility and sense of adventure. Sealed in their transgressive universe, A-listers are liberated from the pressure of maintaining image. Indeed, they are virtually required to act the fool.

By far the best thing about the film, Hanks's Dorr is an eccentric ogre, a gothic aesthete keen to regale Marva Munson (Irma P. Hall) with exemplars of his considerable repertoire of Edgar Allan Poe poetry. Another font of quotes, and another of those pontificating intellectual frauds who bear the brunt of the Coens' apprehension about artistic pretension, he could have slipped straight off the page of a Mark Twain novel. He also bears an uncanny resemblance to chicken-dinner mascot Colonel Sanders

— literature and fast food being two things close to the Coen heart. Dorr is a good example of the multiplicity of high and low culture with which the brothers layer a character. Appearing to have never fully recovered from the loss of The Civil War, Dorr is a Confederate relic situated in the wrong era. One more of those diabolic figures that haunt the margins of Coenesque, only now taking centre stage complete with cane, cape and Van Dyke beard. His name is a derivation of Gustave Doré, the nineteenth-century artist famed for his Dantean engravings with satanic themes. Hanks's sickly sweet accent lightly blends Rhett Butler with Alec Guinness's original huff and puff. And his laugh, a spluttering hairball cough, combines Sylvester the Cat with the Coens' own chorus of wheezing giggles. Like Barton Fink, there is a hint of Coen self-parody about Dorr.

But beyond the eccentric perspicacity of their leading man, the comedy is too broad, even lumbering, lacking the finesse with which the Coens naturally assemble plot and character. The fulminating Hall is more than a match for the inept crooks, something that gnaws away at the concept. She is a devout Southern Baptist and widow, who trucks no 67

# An environment of words: the language of the Coen brothers

While shooting *Raising Arizona* the Coen brothers would take their lunch break at the food counter of the local Woolworths. They liked to listen to conversations at nearby tables, absorbing the cadences of the local accents, the way idle banter took on baffling depths for the uninitiated and suggested a human complexity beneath. Cinematographer Barry Sonnenfeld remembers a story about Ethan and Joel getting into cab outside an airport, where the driver was listening to a sports commentary. 'What's the game?' asked Joel politely. 'Baseball,' the driver replied. They loved that. How perfectly exact and entirely wrong it was. The Coens love how language can be moulded to tell its own stories, how it can deceive as well as reveal. As their plots are assembled from myriad sources, so their synthesis of fictional idioms is made from snatches of real life, accents, odd forms of syntax, personal mantras ('it really tied the room together'), slogans ('you know, for kids'), anecdotes, even songs. The Coens create an environment of words. Through language they find character, and through character they discover worlds. The language is derived in different ways.

The language of genre: the Coens use literary and cinematic pastiche in dialogue as well as imagery. For *Miller's Crossing* they derived an entire gangster patois from genuine phrases of the era and words that simply sounded convincing: 'What's the rumpus?'; 'Are you giving me the high hat?'; 'go dangle'. The idea was to echo the tough-guy slang of 1930s gangster movies, adding to a prefabricated texture, but one so smoothly delivered by the actors it would feel natural. In *The Hudsucker Proxy*, written in a high style of old Hollywood, Jennifer Jason Leigh's Amy Archer rabbits her dialogue in strict adherence to Rosalind Russell's delivery in *His Girl Friday*.

The language of region: both *Raising Arizona* and *Fargo* came under fire for emphasizing distinctive rural accents. It's a fine line, but the unusualness of the local dialect flavours a film, presenting the crime or mishap within the ordinary. The reflexive 'Ja, sure' of Marge's deputy, or the 'kinda funny looking' repeated by the hookers she interrogates in *Fargo* place us in an unsophisticated but redolent world.

Language as character: characters are defined by the way they speak. Mattie Ross in *True Grit* has a didactic tone far beyond her years, hinting at her older self relating the story. Hi's voice-over in *Raising Arizona* is an amalgamation of components: his Arizona accent, a Biblical lilt and spotty self-help information. Bombastic language is put in character's mouths in stark contrast to the circumstances involved: 'You're tasking us to perform this mission?' ascertains Carl Showalter at the beginning of *Fargo* as if going behind enemy lines. Both *The Ladykiller*'s Professor Dorr and *O Brother, Where Art Thou?*'s Everett McGill use language not to convey meaning but to sound clever. *The Big Lebowski*'s The Dude is as inarticulate a character as the Coens have ever written, barely able to muster a coherent sentence, reflecting his generally scatter-brained nature. At times of crisis he repeats lines he has absorbed sponge-like from his environment. 'This aggression will not stand,' he demands, hijacking the words from a George Bush Gulf War commentary on a nearby television set.

The language of comedy: words in a Coen script are often a vehicle for laughs. Here are puns, parroting, smart-aleckry, and characters rising through a thesaurus of descriptions like a musical scale ('Dipstick? Lamebrain? Schmo?' enquires Sydney J. Mussburger of his new employee's probable nicknames in *The Hudsucker Proxy*). In the right mouths profanity swells to hurricanes of unfettered passion. *The Big Lebowski*'s Walter Sobchak feels no need for self-censure, reaching a crescendo of obscenity as he trashes the wrong car: 'This is what happens when you fuck a stranger in the ass!'

The language of capitalism: throughout their films the Coens use the business of marketing and its language of the hard sell. This is as direct as sloganeering ('If you can find lower prices anywhere, my name ain't Nathan Arizona!' rabbits the furniture magnate in *Raising Arizona*), the brand ('I'm a Dapper Dan man,' prevails Everett McGill in *O Brother*) and the crass electioneering of Pappy O'Daniel in *O Brother*.

The language of nomenclature: with a touch of the Dickensian, Coen names are often syncopations of syllables and wordplay suggestive of the origin and nature of their owner. Barton Fink has immediate resonances, a 'fink' being a sneak; Vernon T. Waldrip from *O Brother* is drippy and self-possessed; while Ed Crane of *The Man Who Wasn't There* carries a bird-like quality to his stiff posture.

Tom Hanks in
*The Ladykillers* (2004).

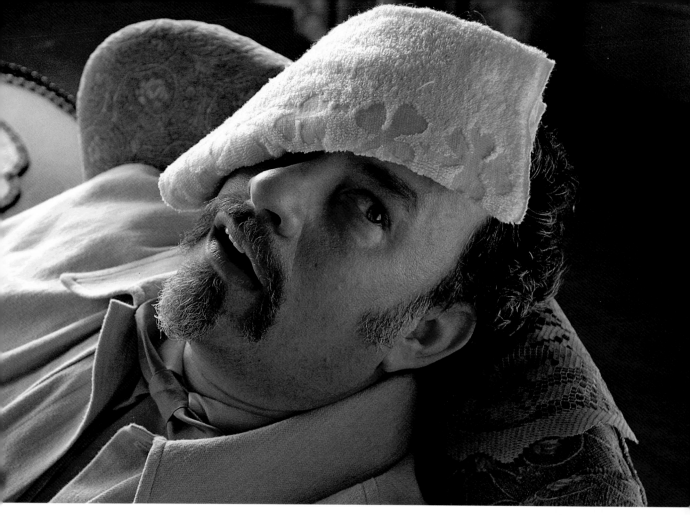

form of cussedness between her four walls, let alone criminal malfeasance. She is, however, prey to the gentle caress of 'art'. Like *Fargo*'s Marge Gunderson, she remains a hardy example of the moral backbone of her gender in the face of male corruption. Profanity is an anathema to Marva, emblematic of disrespectful youth and their immoral 'hippety-hop'. Awkwardly this translates to a racially-centred tension as she fixates on the gang's inside man Gawain (Marlon Wayans) as the focus of her keenest fury. None of the usually rich ancillary characters comes to life. These are the directors' natural comic rhythms played out of time, as if someone else were attempting to replicate their style only to find that Coenesque is impossible to fake.

The critics were aghast, there was no splitting the pack: *The Ladykillers* was universally seen as a genuine, sputtering failure; a film trying too hard. If the Coens have a single purpose, it is to transform all genres into a comic noir. Life's very strangeness

can be portrayed only as black comedy. How do you transform a black comedy into a black comedy?

The Coens dismiss the negativity as no use to them, and at $36 million it hardly counts as the kind of financial failure that *The Hudsucker Proxy* represented. However, *The Ladykillers*, even more so than *Intolerable Cruelty*, feels like an artistic failure. For the first time in the Coens' career their films had become disposable. A three-year gap followed, their longest break from filming, and it is hard not to read it as a chance to rediscover their muse. During this period they briefly returned to make one of the eighteen five-minute 'moments' of *Paris, Je t'aime* (2006), a pluralistic exploration of Paris life made by twenty-two different directors. It marks the only time they have shot away from American soil, although their 'Tuileries' segment features an American tourist, played by Steve Buscemi, who becomes unwittingly involved in a French couple's contretemps.

# The sublime and the ridiculous

## From *No Country for Old Men* to *Burn After Reading*

Brad Pitt in *Burn
After Reading* (2008).

Following pages: Josh Brolin
(on the right) in *No Country
for Old Men* (2007).

### A popular success

Looking as if they had been bitten by a rattlesnake rather than won their second Oscar of the night, the Coens made their way to the stage of the Kodak Theatre. They had already received the award for Best Adapted Screenplay, Joel wryly putting that victory down, having so far only adapted Homer and Cormac McCarthy. Ethan merely muttered, 'Thank you very much'. And now, on the night of 24 February 2008, Martin Scorsese was handing them the prize for Best Direction. Ethan added another brief 'thank you', before Joel told a story from their Super 8 days about how, with Ethan dressed in a suit and carrying a briefcase, they went to Minneapolis International Airport to make a movie about shuttle diplomacy called *Henry Kissinger: Man on the Go*. Joel concluded that what they were doing now honestly didn't feel any different from what they were doing then. By the next category they were winning Best Picture and the Coens didn't say a word. Scott Rudin did all the talking. It was Rudin who had offered McCarthy's novel to the brothers, the first Hollywood producer to parlay Coen obscurantism into popular success. At a cost of $25 million, *No Country for Old Men* (2007) had made $159 million, buoyed by the best reviews of their career.

But to say the Coens had returned to form is misleading. Certainly, after the blow *The Hudsucker Proxy*'s failure had landed on their career (suggesting they didn't have the necessary make-up to upscale from hip indie kids) they regrouped and produced their two most beloved films in *Fargo* and *The Big Lebowski*. They protest to having no antennae for such assessments: each film unto its own. If there are ever regrets, they haven't let them slow them down. And what followed the fallow period of *Intolerable Cruelty* and *The Ladykillers* amounted to a full enrolment into Hollywood entirely on their own terms. The very terms — no interference, final cut, and a predilection to mock the hand that feeds you — that had Orson Welles thrown out of town. Even so, *No Country for Old Men* didn't entirely resemble the Coenesque of old. After all, it was a direct adaptation of a novel. Tuning into strident American literary voices had been a foundation of the Coen philosophy for twenty-three years, but until now they had never directly tackled a novel. Such acidic lyricists as Chandler and Faulkner had provided ambience, plot structure and deplorable character traits for them to exploit. McCarthy is celebrated for his antediluvian characters and the austere grandeur of his Texan border country settings. His extraordinary westerns are symphonies of searing prose, memorializing the hardiest of American mythologies.

No Country for Old Men, which the Coens had read in galley form a year before it was published (2005), was McCarthy's first attempt at a crime thriller, although it could just as easily be considered a neo-western. Set along the shabby Tex-Mex border in 1980, it follows a young hunter who steals a case of money from a crime scene littered with the corpses of Mexican drug dealers. On his tail come a psychotic hitman and an elderly sheriff hoping to restore order before the worst happens; three men brandishing conflicting moral codes. What could be more to the Coens' taste? Its sweeping backdrop echoes the unforgiving landscape of their Midwestern upbringing. It shares the codified male behaviour and spasms of violence of *Miller's Crossing*, a film McCarthy himself deemed 'a very fine picture' — to the brothers' embarrassment. *No Country for Old Men* also recalls *Blood Simple*'s generic Texan milieu and *Fargo*'s unforgettable void. And most alluringly, here too was a chance to examine the cinematic texture of John Ford, Anthony Mann and, most of all, Sam Peckinpah. 'Hard men in the southwest shooting each other — that's definitely Sam Peckinpah's thing', admitted Ethan. [15]

**From The White Sea**

The plot of *No Country for Old Men* was near linear, propelled by a reckless decision along the trajectory of a desperate, vividly realized chase (Joel seriously considered it as their attempt at an 'action movie') that tracked these three figures through the hardscrabble terrain of West Texas. There are passages of action bearing no dialogue, and Carter Burwell's music seems to interchange with the ambient sound. The characters would also correlate with the landscape, and would be portrayed as real human beings, no less. The Coens are often condemned for being heartless, sealed within their own world, where the characters are simply types or nothing more than jokes. But they protest that this is down to the unsympathetic natures of the characters they choose to portray, challenging audiences used to easy, generic Hollywood thinking. And to dismiss their films solely as exercises in ingenious style is to deny the complicated emotions that swirl beneath their slick craftsmanship. In *No Country for*

# 'The disturbed gaze at the authoritarian man': evil in the Coen universe, by Georg Seesslen

Evil exists in Coen films in three very different forms. Firstly, in the very real form of power, power that is generally in the hands of fat, older men, power which is deeply rooted within society and whose continuation is guaranteed by capitalist exploitation and family order. Secondly, in the travails of young protagonists whose desire for something or other brings them into confrontation with the fat, older man. And thirdly, evil exists in the form of a very unreal, murderous projection, in wandering killers and monsters which come into being at the point where the power of the old man meets the desires of the young hero. [...]

Just as the evil fathers' power and conflicting nature appear to be expressed by their names, so too is there in the young losers' monikers a hint of their weakness and their betrayal. A fink is a coward and a traitor, and a dangerously unbalanced lunatic may well be lurking behind Jerry Lundegaard's slowness. In any case, all the young heroes want something and can only get it by challenging paternal power. But they never get what they want. Even if they end up killing the father for it.

A recurring feature in Coen films is the disturbed gaze at the authoritarian man. Barton Fink stares at Hollywood mogul Jack Lipnick. Jerry Lundegaard stares at his father-in-law. Tom Reagan stares at the Irish gang leader. Hi stares at the world of the rich Arizona family and its head. The evil father figure haunts the Coen film universe – he is corpulent and he takes up a lot of space, but the hero is small and weedy and seems just as badly equipped for his Oedipal confrontation as any Kafka creation. The Coen leading man does, however, have one crucial advantage – he is an American.

The strange drama of the Coen film begins with a son forcing his way into the father's territory. Whether he knows it or not, like Oedipus he wants to steal the father's wife, wealth, image and fire (while all the time believing that he is only doing what is expected of him – trying to be successful, to be American). The paternal element – the space of the figure – has of course been anticipating the crime (perhaps has even encouraged it), as he knows all about the ambivalence of women, of power, of image and of fire. (In *Blood Simple* the husband knows that his employee is cuckolding him even before we have seen any adultery take place, and Barnes' fairytale success in *The Hudsucker Proxy* was instigated and manipulated by several rival 'fathers'.)

This is why they do more than merely threaten and plan, and why their conspiracies are all the harder to escape from, because of their powerful positions as bar owners, Hollywood moguls or business tycoons. Above all, they understand the art of deception. (The fact that we only hear Mayhew's worst fits of rage in *Barton Fink* makes us suspect that they could be just as 'real' for him as any performance). The young man does not so much hope to defeat the father (he is often merely seeking affection and recognition) as to simply find his place in the world, but the rage he experiences as he goes through the second birth process leads to another end, to death. Coen films always portray a sort of purgatory.

This is an extract from Georg Seesslen, 'Coen Country' in *Joel & Ethan Coen*, eds Peter Körte and Georg Seesslen, transl. Rory Mulholland, Titan Books, London, 1999.

Left: Javier Bardem in *No Country for Old Men* (2007).

Opposite page: Tommy Lee Jones in *No Country for Old Men* (2007).

Following pages: Javier Bardem (on the right) in *No Country for Old Men* (2007).

*Old Men* characters would be allowed to locate deep-seated emotions, free to be persecuted by the slings and arrows of outrageous fortune. Although, Anton Chigurh is more than a little functional.

## A man caught between heaven and hell

If anything, Chigurh bears an uncanny resemblance to The Terminator, even partaking in a grisly sequence of self-surgery. Javier Bardem, whose physical charisma attracted the directors (they are drawn to bulky actors), described his hitman as machine-like. He appears almost indestructible. Chigurh is deeply, darkly funny, a man who abhors the untidiness of loose ends. He is the devil, made manifest by Moss's rash crime, as psychopathic Charlie Meadows is conjured up by Barton Fink's desperation. Critics of the directors might smirk that he could just as easily serve as the manifestation of the Coen ethos: blackly comic, very violent, no discernable emotions, plus terrible hair. But Chigurh is a creature born of McCarthy's alchemy rather than of the Coens' making. His fiction draws forth such embodiments of nature's essential cruelty, this creature obsessed with the uncertainty of the universe, hanging lives on the toss of a coin. It's a concern the Coens share with McCarthy: that we might be enslaved to a cosmic futility.

Sheriff Bell (Tommy Lee Jones) at least offers a counterpoint. He extols a virtue the film otherwise lacks and is an unusual Coen character in this respect: an upstanding man. If anyone, he recalls Marge Gunderson. Only once they had started shooting, did it occur to the brothers how *No Country for Old Men* resembled *Fargo*: desolate expanses, longeurs of quiet then whirlwinds of dialogue, and a crime committed by an ordinary man escalating out of control. There is also an amusing mirror of Marge's patient interchanges with her slow-witted deputy Lou (Bruce Bohne) in Bell subtly steering his deputy, Wendell (Garret Dillahunt), through their investigation.

The third of the leads, Llewelyn Moss (Josh Brolin), strikes a midpoint between the heaven and hell of Bell and Chigurh (he is sent purgatorial challenges) and proved the toughest to cast. Moss is a decent man, a Vietnam vet (another echo of a distant war) tempted by a cold two million in a suitcase, bringing the devil to his door. The suitcase, like the hat or head-shaped box from past films, serves as the Coen McGuffin.

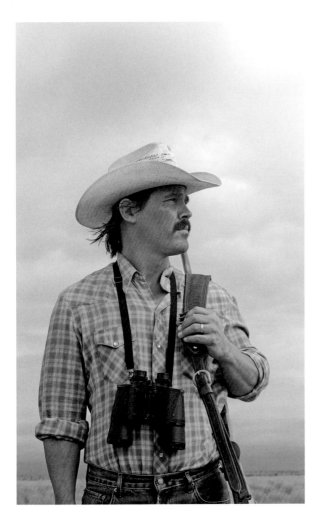

Josh Brolin in *No Country for Old Men* (2007).

Opposite page: Brad Pitt in *Burn After Reading* (2008).

Never had the Coens and Roger Deakins so embraced bleakness as an aesthetic as here, beneath the big skies of New Mexico and West Texas. This is both McCarthy's rough-hewn world and Hollywood's most enduring backcloth: template for a thousand westerns. And in the urban nightscapes, streets splashed in cheap neon, Deakins recalls the oily midnight of *Blood Simple*'s Texas. Such is the rarefied atmosphere of this untameable corner of America, we don't cotton on to the year being 1980: it could be ten years hence, or fifty years before. This isn't realism. The film is reinforcing a mythology rather than deconstructing one. Anthony Lane of *The New Yorker* felt it was 'like a poem adding to an oral tradition'. Why, he wonders, does Moss never simply get on a jet and fly away?[16] Because there is no escaping the archetype, Texas is the entire world. This magnificent, troubling thriller manages the remarkable feat of being both a departure into sincere cinema and another of the Coens' maddeningly brilliant alternative universes. In one darkly comic moment, Moss shoots a rabid hound point blank after it pursues him hilariously down a river. The orchestration of the film, especially its action scenes, carries a cool Coen meticulousness. The desperate, ragged central shoot-out between Moss and Chigurh at the Hotel Earle (a reference to *Barton Fink*'s infernal guesthouse), syncopated to a hail of invisible bullets, inverts the attack on Leo in *Miller's Crossing*, in which the gangster turns the tables on his assailants with almost insouciant grace. The margins of the film are populated with curious kids, grouchy old-timers and a compendium of eccentric locals cast as shopkeepers and receptionists for the value of their regional dialects and Norman Rockwell faces.

**Only without the explosions**

Commentators might have been keen to read it that way, but the uncouth energies of *Burn After Reading* (2008) were not a reaction to winning a hatful of Oscars and being tainted by the establishment. The Coens were well under way with shooting the comedy at the time of the ceremony, much as they had been shooting *The Big Lebowski* at the time *Fargo* won its awards. Instead, this was another comedy founded on the juxtaposition of incongruent elements: international espionage and internet dating, personal training and sexual deviancy. Ethan

half-seriously decided it was their version of a Jason Bourne or Tony Scott type movie, 'only without the explosions'. [17] And even though they disavowed any link to contemporary issues, it was impossible not to draw a connection with Bush-era paranoia: how the concept of national security had reached fever pitch among America's citizenry. Rather than concentrating on a duo or trio of protagonists, this was an ensemble comedy in the manner of 1970s satirists Robert Altman or Hal Ashby. And, despite being set in a contemporary Washington, D.C., the film has the crisp, realistic look of '70s thrillers such as *Three Days of the Condor* and *All the President's Men*, only with conspiracy served up as absurdist comedy. One they had written around specific faces and body shapes, knowing exactly who they wanted to cast in what was effectively a farce.

The epicentre of the plot's chain reaction of events is a low-ranking CIA data analyst named Ozzie Cox (John Malkovich), a number cruncher likely inspired by Ethan's early employment as a statistical typist at Macy's in New York. Ozzie has a drink problem. Ozzie also has anger management issues. He's another fraying personality at the opposite extreme of the composed Coen brothers. Demoted, he quits in a fit of pique, determined to write an incendiary memoir exposing his former employers. Into Ozzie's orbit come two unwise employees (Frances McDormand and Brad Pitt) of Hardbodies Fitness Center (a further vain anathema to the directors), who happen upon a computer disk of his notes left in the ladies changing rooms, take it for high-level intelligence and try to sell the 'drivel' to the Russians, even though the Cold War has been over for years. Linda Litzke, the (ever-so) slightly smarter of the two, was another 'gift' for Frances McDormand. However, rather than the chirpy grace of Marge Gunderson, McDormand

was required to bring all her talent for body language and willingness to play dowdy to Linda, this vulgar buffoon, like Dot from *Raising Arizona*, determined to fund her plastic surgery. Linda also comes short on sentiment. In fact, on first view, this entire 'league of morons' runs the gamut from unsympathetic to repellent. Circling them is Harry Pfarrer (George Clooney), a homeland security agent preoccupied both by a dwindling affair with Ozzie's faithless wife Katie (Tilda Swinton) and hooking up with the eager Linda via a dating site. He is an unctuous swine, jittery with hypochondria and paranoid delusions, who has built some unspeakable apparatus in his basement (a joke about gym machines).

The script hungrily divests its stars of their charm, stretching them into blackly comic situations that the Hollywood formula would deny them. Joel insisted they don't make distinctions between actors and comedians. [18] It is how the character looks and sounds that is important, how he or she fits the Coen concept. But given half a chance, those brothers do love to mock celebrity culture.

## The meaning of meaninglessness

*Burn After Reading* is also sending up Americans' myopic view of the world. It is the little man rather than the bureaucrats in the directors' crosshairs. The office-bound CIA and Russian suits are benign and rather gormless, mostly seen as a pair of hurried heels scuttling along the polished floors of officialdom (tracking after feet is a characteristic Coen motif). Both the CIA's headquarters at Langley and the glum Soviet-era Russian embassy are depicted as drab and functional.

Outside, it is a placid, autumnal picture of fallen leaves and colonial Georgetown houses. An overly preened and ageing city, created from locations in New York State and New Jersey. For all the intrigue that engulfs them, these are characters without much meaning in their lives, hence their need to manufacture drama. Again, the characters are writing their own stories, from adulteries to memoirs to the silly children's books written by Harry's wife. Paradoxically, Ozzie was just a penpusher at the CIA. He has no scandal to invest in

Opposite page: Frances McDormand in *Burn After Reading* (2008).

Right: George Clooney in *Burn After Reading* (2008).

his memoirs, while Linda and Harry are also creating fictional lives for their dating profiles. Moreover, Harry is convinced he is being followed, but can't figure out which agency might be doing so. Stories lie within stories like Russian dolls and, as with *The Big Lebowski* or *Blood Simple*, no one has a firm grasp on reality. 'Report back to me... when it makes sense', commands J. K. Simmons's desk-bound CIA superior. The entire meaning of the film circles the idea that meaning can be a facade.

But some critics found the film too caustic. There was no warmth to offset the ignorance and selfishness. No Marge or Dude. Yet the lack of sympathy is deceptive. Between the lurches of botched espionage there is pathos. Here is a collection of cranks undone by middle age, terrified of irrelevance in a changing world (with the added resonance of movie stars confronting age: 'I would be laughed out of Hollywood', smirks Linda of her figure). Linda wants to update her body, renew herself; Harry clings to his youth through sexual conquest; and Ozzie is fooling himself he is some romantic Cold War warrior.

What we see as conspiracy is actually the tawdry fall-out from failing marriages, affairs and forlorn attempts to muster excitement in later life. Hence the sideways references to President Clinton's indiscretions: Linda's severe fringe is based on Monica Lewinsky's confidante Linda Tripp, while Harry beds a lady named 'Monica'. The film repeatedly shows us older bodies straining to exercise themselves back into youth. In that there is tragedy.

This is an appropriate time to consider the middle age of the Coen career. Has there been a discernable maturity? Such was the thoroughness of their filmmaking from its inception that their 'corner of the sandbox' has shown little outward modulation. Changing themes, a different sense of the world, have emerged; a gradient towards older characters and the concerns of age. Similarly toned comedies *Raising Arizona* and *Burn After Reading* are demonstrably films made by young and older men; while *Blood Simple* is less polished a noir than *No Country for Old Men*. The interesting question is: were they getting more personal? Were we getting closer to the Coens?

# Predictably unpredictable

From *A Serious Man* to *True Grit*

Michael Stuhlbarg in
*A Serious Man* (2009).

## Equal opportunity hecklers

Growing up in the suburban enclave of St. Louis Park, the Coens were the only Jewish family on the block. Their parents were both orthodox, but it was their mother who was the stickler — a legacy from her folks who came from Riga in Latvia — and refused even to drive on the Sabbath. It was she who ensured the young brothers maintained tradition. Both had bar mitzvahs, observed religious holidays, attended Hebrew school, and were grounded in the tapestry of rules and regulations that envelops Judaism. The brothers are regular American contradictions. Their natural Minnesotan reserve is liberated by a Jewish volubility, as their Jewish volubility is restrained by their Minnesotan reserve. They have been markedly fascinated by the place of Jews in art and entertainment. They toy with stereotypes, filling their scripts with epithets at their own expense: 'schmattes', 'Hebrews' and 'kikes'. Accusations of masochistically singling out Jews feel moot — they are no more vilified than numerous other ethnic, social and religious groups. The Coens are equal-opportunity hecklers. And how is this different from Martin Scorsese and Francis Ford Coppola's exploration and often criticism of their Italian roots? Gentiles are keen enough to enrol. Both Leo in *Miller's Crossing* and Walter in *The Big Lebowski* have taken vows. Concepts of assimilation and depictions of diverse subcultures (ghettos of ethnic, regional, cultural and vocational minorities) suffuse their work. Everywhere we turn there are tribes.

The Coens' Jewish heritage has been a major influence on Coenesque. Hoisted by their own irony, this makes them highly personal filmmakers. So much so there is often a nagging sensation we are intruding on a private joke. However, a willingness to actually set a film in a Minnesotan Jewish community of the late 1960s, the subculture of their own youth, was a welcome surprise. Not that it would be at the expense of their off-centre vision. *A Serious Man* (2009) was to be their most oblique film since *Barton Fink* and was a return to small-scale production ($7 milllion).

If *O Brother, Where Art Thou?* was partially drawn from *The Odyssey*, then *A Serious Man* is a rewriting of the Book of Job. We will share in the series of travails that befall Larry Gopnik (Michael Stuhlbarg), a physics professor and, or so he thought, a contentedly married father of two. Things will get bad for Larry: his upcoming

Joel Coen and Ethan Coen with Aaron Wolff (centre) on the set of *A Serious Man* (2009).

tenure looks on shaky ground, a student is trying to bribe him, his redneck neighbour is encroaching on his lawn, his wife has announced she is leaving him for smooth-talking serious man Sy Ableman (Fred Melamed), and his unmanly brother Arthur (Richard Kind) has moved in along with his sebaceous cyst. This last component suggests the plague of boils that is afflicted upon Job. A plot device, like the 'head in a box' in *Barton Fink*, we never glimpse. Larry doesn't deserve his fate. He is a good man, an ethical man, he hopes even a serious man. Which, from what we can tell, pertains to a dedicated mix of piety and standing in the community. It's another incarnation of idealized manhood a Coen man will fail to attain. That signature warning: striving to be a serious man is a vain pursuit.

## God versus science

Rather than a voice-over easing us into the plot's conundrums, we begin with a self-contained folktale voiced entirely in Yiddish (hence those early auditions), and told with the wry provincialism of Isaac Bashevis Singer or Sholem Aleichem, even a touch of Kafka. In a snowy nineteenth-century Polish shtetl, a dybbuk may have come to visit a bickering peasant couple. The tricky business is this malevolent spirit seems to be disguised as recently deceased community elder Reb Groshkover from Lodz. While it appears to have no link with the ensuing narrative (or could they be long-distant Gopnik ancestors?), like many previous narrators or faked title cards, it is there to set a tone. However everyday the body of the film appears, it too is the progeny of folklore, where good men are prey to

Michael Stuhlbarg and Fred Melamed in *A Serious Man* (2009).

the machinations of storytellers. The question is, did Larry bring his curse upon himself or has the universe got it in for him? In other words, why do the Jews have all the bad luck? Or why is it the Jews always complain (with some reason) about having all the bad luck?

Larry is certainly a contradiction: a devout man and a physicist. He can fill a blackboard with the dauntingly complex calculations behind the Heisenberg Uncertainty Principle (making its second appearance in the Coen canon; they like how it seems to sum up humankind's predicament), but still wants God to answer his querulous calls. Neither science nor religion is doing him much good. He tries to be a serious man, but his life is a joke. He is in search of answers from the cosmos, from his wife Judith (Sari Lennick), most of all from

the trilogy of rabbis he turns to for solace. But everywhere he turns the riddle deepens.

Like *Fargo*, the characters offer a gathering of ordinary at its most outlandish, and again the directors encourage nuanced performances from their actors, transcending caricature. And for all the Coens' deft comedy, the film is defined by Stuhlbarg's moving performance. Larry is a model of fraying fortitude, his eyebrows wearily lifting heavenwards at each new injustice, helplessly appealing for sanity to be restored. He is key to the film's universality. Larry's is not just a Jewish condition; it is the human condition.

### The personal touch

With no little irony, Larry's increasing frustration starts to resemble an intrepid journalist trying to  85

# Solo Coen

Rarely interviewed apart, the Coen brothers are generally spoken about as a single creative unit, providing little insight into their different sensibilities. Even the initial distinction of Ethan as producer and Joel as director proved arbitrary: they do both together, the work being entirely collaborative. At the writing stage it is true that Ethan types (as the better typist), while during editing, Joel (who learned his trade in the cutting room) cuts and splices. Curiously, storyboard artist J. Todd Anderson noticed that they tended to see shots from opposite directions: Ethan from left to right, Joel from right to left. Ethan is more likely to become infected by a phrase, chasing it round his head until it lands in a screenplay (he insisted on 'take your flunky and dangle' in *Miller's Crossing*). Tellingly, it is also Ethan who has pursued his muse beyond the films, publishing plays, short stories and poetry. He blithely considers these a recreation, whereas directing films is the day job, but they provide us with a picture of him as a stand-alone artist.

In 1998 Ethan published *Gates of Eden*, a collection of short stories, an entertaining aggregation of recognizably Coen tropes: down-on-their-heels private eyes, alcoholics, cops, bar tenders, radio jocks and pernickety Jewish kids. It is a frenetic mix of noir parody and whimsical homages to his Minnesotan upbringing that read like microcosms of the films, suggesting that Ethan is largely responsible for the sulphuric wit, existential undertow and intricate cadences of speech. There is certainly a delight in bending language to humour: in one story a blind client communicates with a deaf investigator by typewriter, only his hands are wrongly positioned, informing the detective 'U tgubj nt mufe us cgeatubg ub ne'. Yet, in his deconstruction of formula, he reveals human frailty. Something amplified in *The Drunken Driver Has the Right of Way*, a collection of his poetry from 2009 (a second collection, *The Day the World Ends*, was published in 2012). Again, the worlds he crafts are familiar: weird Americana, scalding violence, tough-guy dialogue and the junking of film noir. He toys with rhymes and limericks, mocking the notion of poetry as high art, while picking over heroes like Dashiell Hammett, William Faulkner and Jean-Paul Sartre. Ethan's verse cleaves closer to pathos, there is an aura of disappointment and evaporating dreams. 'Toppled in the Street' heartbreakingly depicts an old man contemplating his mortality from the asphalt as strangers gawp at his frail, fading body. The effect of the movies is intensified on the page; a pall of existential dread hangs over the mordant humour and lightly worn cleverness.

Ethan's career as a dramatist debuted with an Off-Broadway production of his triptych of miniature plays *Almost an Evening* in 2008. Reviewers greeted the three sketches warmly, enjoying the cosmic jokes and wafts of Samuel Beckett, a surrealist quality that has been ascribed to the brothers' films. Here the Coens' estranged USA is transfigured into a metaphysical universe where enlightenment is an empty quest, reminding us that it is Ethan who has the master's degree in philosophy.

Michael Stuhlbarg in
*A Serious Man* (2009).

elicit answers from the enigmatic Coens. 'Why does he make us feel the questions, if he's not going to give us the answers?', implores Larry. Why indeed? Should he just sit back and embrace the mystery? Naturally, when the question of autobiography came up in interview, the brothers were circumspect at best. You could say it was *reminiscent* of their childhoods.

Danny (Aaron Wolff), Larry's son, represents the growing tension in the late 1960s between the lure of the secular world being fed to the young through their unreliable television sets and the archaic values being thrust upon them by their elders. All the film's scrupulous cultural details ring of personal experience: the Red Owl grocery store, *F Troop*, and the Columbia Record Club Danny has signed up to behind Larry's back. Among the manifold tribulations piling at his door, Larry is about to receive a copy of Santana's *Abraxas* album. It's the singularity of the choice that makes it so perfect. The tartness of memory. Music will play its part, mixing Carter Burwell's elegiac score, infused with Judaic harmonics, with the psychedelic rock of Jefferson Airplane: another indication of tradition squabbling with the future.

The Midwestern setting is as lovely and drab as Fargo, with that sense of something threatening lurking beneath the placid surface. Making his

Aaron Wolff in *A Serious Man* (2009).

return, cinematographer Roger Deakins uses odd tilts, shifting focal points and low-slung tracking shots to warp normality, as if the entire world is stoned. Here is a treacherous ordinariness where every ringing phone is prelude to a new catastrophe. And while divested of immediate Coen violence, this is as unsettling as anything they have done.

Nonetheless, *A Serious Man* helps make sense of many of the brothers' so-called enigmas. How the interminable rituals of their Jewish upbringing are echoed in their obsession with the moral mechanics of their chosen worlds: endless ethics, laws and ceremonial behaviours. Ignore them at your peril. Larry is the most acute example of a Coen character tormented by self-realization. It is those who question their place who are punished. The Dude will be beaten and robbed for taking on the investigation; Norville Barnes driven to suicide when he learns he is a proxy; Carl Showalter shot, axed and fed into a wood chipper for daring to apply logic to *Fargo*. Question God, the universe or the Coens and you invite trouble. The story is inviolate, the script sacrosanct. Laugh or die. It also emerges how much their style bears the salty, kvetching, philosophical timbre of an old-time Jewish comedian — a vein of self-mockery running from Woody Allen to Jackie Mason. That love of telling a good yarn, often heavily coloured,

Joel Coen and Ethan Coen on the set of *A Serious Man* (2009).

# The serious man trilogy

*Barton Fink* (1991), *The Man Who Wasn't There* (2001) and *A Serious Man* (2009) complete an individual trilogy within the body of the Coens' work. Each of these films circles the forlorn attempts of three highly contrasting yet comparable men to bring their chaotic worlds (or whatever their directors might want to throw at them) under control. More than their other films, they are character pieces, albeit centred on characters who are notably self-absorbed, introspective and tormented. Two are Jewish, the other an alien of his own kind. An increasingly bizarre universe confronts each man. A world that slips into the supernatural as a single challenge is made of them. A challenge that will prove insurmountable.

John Turturro's playwright Barton Fink is a serious artist asked simply to write a wrestling picture for a Hollywood studio, but he becomes stricken with writer's block and begins to manifest evils in the fabric of his hotel, most strikingly the 'common man' of his dreams: a psychopathic insurance salesman in the room next door. Billy Bob Thornton's barber Ed Crane – the least intellectual of the three but still quite a thinker – merely wants to get into 'dry cleaning', but his attempts will be beset by murder and otherworldly visions of UFOs. He will be the least reactive and least tormented by his circumstances (as the least clever), but will lose everything. Michael Stuhlbarg's Larry Gopnik is a physics professor who only wants to gain tenure at his small-town university, to be thought of as a 'serious man' in his community, but he will face trial after trial sent from an indifferent God. He is undeserving, but the trap it appears is that desire to improve yourself in some way, to be thought of as a better man. Each 'serious man', in different ways, is seeking out the American Dream (Barton wants both artistic recognition and the rewards of Hollywood). According to the Coens, this is not quite as available as its reputation suggests. Moreover, each film hovers poetically between comedy and tragedy. These are the brothers' most becalmed films, and arguably their most personal and precious. The Coens too are serious men.

often going off at wild tangents, before hitting you with a punchline and crumpling into gurgles of laughter. The Coens make entire films as long, complicated, insightful jokes. This isn't nihilism. They take their characters to the edge of sanity, to discover that humanity clings on. Tom Reagan keeps his hat, Hi dreams of Utah, and The Dude goes bowling …

Without big names, and loaded with ambiguities, *A Serious Man* played to a more select audience, but being inexpensive, its $31 million worldwide was a healthy reward, as were two Academy Award nominations: Best Original Screenplay and Best Picture. Critics now sounded like long-time fans, delighted the Coens had returned to the elliptical strengths of their early work. But with an added human dimension.

What, though, are we to make of the elusive ending? Just as harmony is restored, Larry's phone rings again and Danny looks up to see a twister spinning in his direction, another punishment from God or Oz or the Coens. Out of their most personal film comes their bleakest conclusion: there is no escape… Still, those who stayed for the credits might yet have smiled at the disclaimer: 'No Jews were harmed in the making of this motion picture.' Laugh or die.

## Seeking the right voice

After the throwback of *A Serious Man*, the Coens hungered for something bigger. They decided to make *True Grit* (2010), not a remake of the John Wayne hit of 1969 but an adaptation of the original novel by Charles Portis published in 1968.

While sharing his dark humour and craggy vistas, Charles Portis is a more playful and romantic writer than Cormac McCarthy, and closer to the Coen sensibility. The brothers had been attracted to a kindred spirit. He is as equally drawn to the oddness in folk. His knack for a name and unconventional turn of plot carry the Coenesque patina. And he shares their ear for the seesawing, literary

Michael Stuhlbarg in
*A Serious Man* (2009).

cadences of American speech. Among the many lures of *True Grit* was a chance to portray another community isolated — historically and geographically — and enriched with its own peculiar vernacular. The way *Miller's Crossing* is defined by its gangster argot or *O Brother, Where Art Thou?* by its hiccuping hayseed dialect.

The novel is narrated by the warm fastidiousness of Mattie's voice: stalwart, particular to the syllable, and fuming with moral righteousness and a facility for lending her arguments quotes from the King James Bible. Out of the thousands they auditioned, ninety-nine per cent didn't get close to that rich voice, but a fourteen-year-old from Thousand Oaks, Los Angeles, named Hailee Steinfeld appeared to have walked straight out of the 1870s. She was a natural with the script's old-time phrasing, much of it taken verbatim from the novel. In fact, Steinfeld was far more adept than her seasoned co-stars. By contrast, Bridges' Rooster chews and slurs his conversation, barely audible — a whiskey-drinking, tobacco-spitting,

Below: Matt Damon and Hailee Steinfeld in *True Grit* (2010).

Opposite page: Jeff Bridges in *True Grit* (2010).

frontier-country Dude. That is until he trains his gun upon any feckless dolt who crosses him. Then he turns cold, skilful; a killer of distinction. How often Coen characters appear ill equipped for everything but meting out death! Bridges worked hard on dropping his contractions ('don't' had to be 'do not'; 'can't' had to be 'cannot'), letting the heavy words carry their own weight. Barry Pepper, who plays gang leader Lucky Ned Pepper, thought of his lines as American Shakespeare complete with iambic pentameters, rhythm and musicality. Everyone in *True Grit* is in love with the sound of his or her own voice, but no one is quite as uncorked as Matt Damon's LaBoeuf, who lectures the world with his drawling braggadocio, wryly punctuated by draws on his pipe. Of course, there was to be no improvisation. All these peculiar inflections were entirely defined by the script.

## Hit and myth

The plot may have been situated in Arkansas, where Portis was born, but the Coens were unusually content to cheat and find somewhere archetypal rather than precise. They scouted Oklahoma, Tennessee and Utah, but settled for New Mexico as it instantly recalled the countryside of John Ford's *The Searchers* (1956), Howard Hawks's *Red River* (1948) and Henry Hathaway's original version of *True Grit*. Something classically western, more lush and wooded than the rugged deserts of *No Country for Old Men*. The film seems to pass through the seasons in illogical order and haste: autumn, summer, winter, before alighting in a crisp spring for the showdown. Once beyond the bricks and mortar of Fort William, re-created from old photographs, the wilds of the reservation take on a surreal complexion as if the riders have passed into legend. Which to an extent they have. 93

Like the trio of vagrants of *O Brother, Where Art Thou?*, the three wanderers will encounter every manner of oddity, most true to Portis's novel. Although, the aged dentist wrapped in a bearskin comes direct from the imaginations of Joel and Ethan; the brothers are partial to doctors and dentists. The trajectory is from urban realism into rustic yarn, dissolving entirely into fable for the dramatic conclusion as Rooster races through a star-dappled night to save Mattie from a snake bite.

*True Grit* proved a thundering success, the first Coen film to cross the $100 million mark in the USA (it made $250 million worldwide). Reviewers noted a lack of Coenesque trickery, that after *A Serious Man* the directors had made their least personal and most accessible film. Was its popularity more about Mattie's appealing stridency (it is she who proves to have 'true grit') than the brothers' filmmaking? Certainly the film can be taken at face value, even deemed heartfelt. There is a tenderness to the father-daughter bond that forms between Rooster and Mattie, even as their performances remain unsentimental, two souls hardened by their times. The film is truer to a movie tradition, there is less deconstruction, no rewiring of genre. For all its talking, it had less to say. It was just a film. If it was Coenesque, that was as much down to Portis's style: the language, the black humour, the astringent violence, all these American staples in sharp focus. Were audiences at last able to have their cake and eat it? To be transported into a film and not be reminded they were sitting a cinema, and still savour the verve and imagination of the Coens' filmmaking? In that there was something a little sad.

Hailee Steinfeld, Matt Damon and Jeff Bridges in *True Grit* (2010).

Joel Coen and Ethan Coen
with Jeff Bridges on the set
of *True Grit* (2010).

## O brothers

The Coens represent something impossible: a direc-
torial career entirely of their own design, where
they have retained final cut, creating a hermeti-
cally sealed world in which they can foster their
own muse, untempered by fashion, market forces or
studio pressure. Somewhere that reconstructs tradition, but whose motive is unclear. Come triumph
or turkey, they have not wavered. After twenty-nine
years and fifteen feature films, they have become
an institution. Their legion fans are unconcerned
by what they choose to do next, only in the result.
All we seek is the next intricate Coenesque palace

of dreams and violence populated with fast-talking dames and faster-talking heels flat out of luck, where emotion eternally struggles with ironic gesture and black comedy, where meaning and truth will slip from our grasp like catching smoke; films that will tempt us to unpick their knotted puzzles.

It is the questions that are important. Writing, directing, producing and editing their films, the Coens come as close as any filmmakers to fulfilling *auteur* theory, albeit one conjoined across two minds. However, a final definition of Coenesque remains elusive. And that is as it should be. The brothers themselves may not know what it is. They reconfigure myth as a means of revelation. And through their stylization, so tiered with references and built from recurrent themes and devices, a shared DNA, they have discovered an America not found anywhere else — this dark, funny and peculiar map of the human predicament. All their irony and cleverness are not reductive, they are born out of this spirit of enquiry, an enquiry into the fabric of storytelling itself. Within that, there is self-analysis. From dreams to songs to myths, to their own medium — film: here they display their knowledge and impart something of themselves. These fifteen films are also a map of Joel and Ethan Coen.

# Chronology

### 1954
**29 November.** Joel Daniel Coen is born in Minneapolis, Minnesota, to Ed and Rena Coen, and is younger brother to Deborah Ruth Coen.

### 1957
**21 September.** Ethan Jesse Coen is born in Minneapolis, Minnesota. The Coen family are of Polish-Russian-Jewish extraction, their paternal grandfather having shortened an elaborate Polish cognomen to Coen as it sounded more Irish.

### 1965
Joel buys their first Super 8 camera in order for the brothers to make films with their gang of local friends. The fruit of their endeavours includes *Ed … A Dog*, *The Banana Film*, *Lumberjacks of the North* and *Henry Kissinger: Man on the Go*.

### 1968
Both brothers attend high school teacher Pete Peterson's extracurricular film class The Eight and A Half Club, where among much world cinema they see François Truffaut's *The 400 Blows* for the first time. Otherwise, both brothers are equally viewed as 'unremarkable' students.

### 1974
**Autumn.** Joel enrols in the undergraduate film course at the Tisch School of the Arts at New York University. After four years he joins the graduate film school at The University of Texas at Austin. His choice is governed by a short early marriage. He lasts only a semester in Austin, but it provides inspiration for the setting of *Blood Simple*.

Joel Coen on the set of *Blood Simple* (1984).

### 1977
**Autumn.** Ethan, having no real idea of what he wants to pursue, opts to go to Princeton to study philosophy. He completes his thesis 'Two Views of Wittgenstein's Later Philosophy'. In a nascent display of Coen irony the paper uses Wittgenstein to criticize the Wittgensteinian.

### 1980
**Spring.** Ethan moves in with his brother in New York, and earns much needed cash by writing part-time on the television cop show *Cagney & Lacey*. The brothers begin to collaborate on scripts with the intention of making their own film. Among these early screenplays is a film noir called *Blood Simple* set in Texas. Debutant director Sam Raimi hires Joel as assistant editor on his horror movie *The Evil Dead* (with Edna Ruth Paul as head editor). Raimi, as well as influencing the brothers' style and becoming a key collaborator, funds his first film via local investors, which motivates the Coens to do the same when they come to finance *Blood Simple*.

### 1982
**4 October.** The eight-week shoot begins on *Blood Simple* in and around Austin, Texas. Joel is twenty-seven years old, Ethan twenty-five. During the shoot Joel begins a relationship with actress Frances McDormand, who plays the film's female lead, Abby.

### 1983
While trying to land distribution for *Blood Simple* and living in Los Angeles with Sam Raimi, the Coens meet Ben Barenholtz of Circle Films. So impressed is Barenholtz by their debut film that he agrees to distribute it and signs them up on a four-picture deal. The brothers also begin collaborating on two scripts with Raimi: *The XYZ Murders* and *The Hudsucker Proxy*.

Joel Coen and Ethan Coen on the set of *Raising Arizona* (1987).

### 1984
**1 April.** Joel marries Frances McDormand. Sam Raimi directs the comic crime caper *The XYZ Murders*, which flops under the title *Crimewave* (1985). The Coens later disown the project, but its zany, hyperkinetic style prefigures *Raising Arizona*, which they are currently writing.

### 1985
**18 January.** Having premiered at the Sundance Film Festival to critical acclaim, *Blood Simple* opens on a very limited release to become a small-scale hit. On the back of their success the Coens move out of Hollywood and return to New York.

### 1986
**January.** Filming begins on the thirteen-week shoot for *Raising Arizona*.

### 1987
**February.** As *Raising Arizona* has its first screening in New York, the Coens are attending a screening of Sam Raimi's *The Evil Dead 2*. Asked why they weren't at their own film, Joel replied, 'We've seen that one.' **6 March.** *Raising Arizona* is released in the USA, becoming a sizeable hit.

### 1988
The Coens are offered and turn down the chance to make *Batman* for Warner Brothers. Instead they pitch a period gangster thriller called *Miller's Crossing* to Circle Films and 20th Century Fox. While stuck with the writing of *Miller's Crossing*, they go to Los Angeles. The trip inspires the script for *Barton Fink*, the first draft of which they finish in three weeks. Writing *Barton Fink* frees up *Miller's Crossing*, which they now complete. They also manage to include some uncredited rewrites on Sam Raimi's *Darkman* into their schedule.

Joel Coen and Ethan Coen on the set of *Fargo* (1996).

### 1989
**Autumn.** Shooting begins on *Miller's Crossing* in New Orleans.

### 1990
**27 June.** The forty-five-day shoot starts on *Barton Fink* in a bar on *The Queen Mary* in Long Beach, Los Angeles. As Barry Sonnenfeld has moved on to directing, they hire Roger Deakins, forming a pivotal creative partnership with the British cinematographer. **21 September.** *Miller's Crossing* opens the prestigious New York Film Festival to generous reviews. **2 October.** Ethan marries editor Tricia Cooke.

### 1991
**May.** *Barton Fink* premieres at the Cannes Film Festival, where head of the jury Roman Polanski, perhaps enjoying similarities with his own work, helps award it the Palme d'Or and Best Actor for John Turturro. **21 August.** *Barton Fink* opens in the USA to good reviews and moderate returns.

### 1992
The Coens tidy up the dormant script for *The Hudsucker Proxy*, written with Sam Raimi in 1984. Meanwhile, they begin work on two new scripts entitled *Fargo* and *The Big Lebowski*. In their own distinctive ways both are crime stories. **November.** The demanding fifteen-week shoot for *The Hudsucker Proxy* begins at the Carolco Studios in Wilmington, North Carolina, with Sam Raimi acting as second-unit director.

### 1994
**January.** *The Hudsucker Proxy* gets a muted response at the Sundance Film Festival. **11 March.** It flops badly both critically and commercially on its US release. It is the first serious damage done to the Coens' burgeoning career. Undaunted, the brothers turn to *The Big Lebowski* as their next film, but with Jeff Bridges busy filming, swiftly move on to *Fargo*.

### 1995
**23 January.** Filming begins on *Fargo* in an unseasonably warm Minnesota winter, leaving them short of the desired snowfall.

## 1996

**8 March.** *Fargo* opens on limited release in the USA, giving the Coens the best reviews of their career. **11 April.** Going wide, it becomes their biggest hit since *Raising Arizona*. This proves a productive time for the brothers as later the same year Joel and Frances McDormand go to Paraguay to adopt a son, Pedro, and Ethan and Tricia Cooke give birth to a son, Buster. They also start toying with an idea for resetting Homer's *The Odyssey* in Depression-era Mississippi, later called *O Brother, Where Art Thou?*, and a full adaptation of James Dickey's *To The White Sea*.

## 1997

**24 March.** Out of seven nominations, *Fargo* wins two Oscars at the Academy Awards: Best Actress for Frances McDormand and Best Original Screenplay for Joel and Ethan. During the lead up to the event, the Coens are forced to confess their nominated editor Roderick Jaynes is in fact a pseudonym for themselves.

## 1998

**15 February.** *The Big Lebowski* debuts at the Berlin International Film Festival, before underwhelming at the America box office when it opens on 6 March. A groundswell of appreciation for the Jeff Bridges comedy thriller begins, and will make it the most popular of all Coen films. **November.** Ethan releases a collection of fourteen short stories as *Gates of Eden*, many of which had been previously published in *Playboy*, *Vanity Fair* and *The New Yorker*. This mix of familiar noirish parodies and crime capers receives good reviews. Together the brothers adapt Elmore Leonard's *Cuba Libre* and do a rewrite of a romantic comedy called *Intolerable Cruelty*, both for Universal.

Joel Coen and Ethan Coen on the set of *O'Brother* (2000).

## 1999

**August.** Shooting begins on *O Brother, Where Art Thou?* in and around Canton, Mississippi.

## 2000

**13 May.** *O Brother, Where Art Thou?* premieres at the Cannes Film Festival, going on to become a hit on an international roll out, before opening in the USA as late as 22 December. While promoting the movie, the Coens mention they are about to start filming 'The Barber Project', starring Billy Bob Thornton, that is filmed in Santa Rosa and the suburbs of Los Angeles, California.

## 2001

**May.** *The Man Who Wasn't There* becomes the latest Coen film to be asked to compete at the Cannes Film Festival, where Joel shares the award for Best Director with David Lynch for *Mulholland Drive*.

## 2002

**Spring.** About to go into production on wartime survival drama *To The White Sea* with Brad Pitt, 20th Century Fox rationalizes the budget to a level where the brothers no longer feel their film is sustainable and the project is cancelled. Instead, they accept the offer to direct *Intolerable Cruelty* in Los Angeles through the summer. Ostensibly a studio project, it is their most expensive film ever: ironically, at $60 million, exactly the budget they required for *To The White Sea*.

## 2003

**2 September.** *Intolerable Cruelty* debuts at the Venice Film Festival. The reception is mixed, but it does well on its US release on 10 October, by which time, the fertile Coens have already wrapped production on *The Ladykillers*, their first official remake.

## 2004

**26 March.** *The Ladykillers* opens to poor reviews, the general feeling being that it is another studio-derived product rather than a true representation of the Coen talents. Alongside *Intolerable Cruelty*, this is deemed a creative low point in their career. Significantly or not, due to a new ruling at the Directors Guild of America, this is the first time they share credit for directing, writing and producing. While continuing work on various scripts, the Coens take their time before going back into production.

## 2005

**August** .The Coens agree to direct an adaptation of Cormac McCarthy's neo-western *No Country for Old Men*.

## 2007

**27 August.** Heading back to their knockabout roots, they shoot the black comedy *Burn After Reading*. It is their first original screenplay since *The Man Who Wasn't There*. **9 November.** *No Country for Old Men* opens on limited release in the USA, where the ecstatic reviews signal a welcome return to form for the Coens, a view backed up by eight Academy Award nominations.

## 2008

**24 February.** *No Country for Old Men* picks up four awards: Best Supporting Actor (for Javier Bardem), Best Adapted Screenplay, and the 'big two' – Best Director and Best Picture. **8 September.** The Coens begin shooting their third film in a row – a small-scale, highly personal comedy-drama set in a Minneapolis suburb, entitled *A Serious Man*. **12 October.** Following its premiere at the Venice Film Festival, *Burn After Reading* opens in the USA.

## 2009

**2 October.** *A Serious Man* is widely viewed as the Coens' most autobiographical work, depicting a Jewish community at the tail end of the 1960s. While box-office returns are moderate, the film is nominated as Best Picture and is deemed a required sister piece to the ambiguities of *Barton Fink*. The Coens are already deep into an adaptation of Charles Portis's western novel *True Grit*, something they have been considering since 2008.

Joel Coen and Ethan Coen on the set of *A Serious Man* (2009).

## 2010

**March.** Production begins on *True Grit* in Santa Fe, New Mexico, and barring a few weather problems goes smoothly to completion in June. **22 December.** *True Grit* is released in the USA and becomes a huge hit, grossing $250 million worldwide.

## 2011

**May.** The Coen-scripted remake of *Gambit*, directed by Michael Hoffman, goes into production. After a well-earned break, the brothers begin considering what to do next, eventually announcing a project called *Inside Llewyn Davis*, set in New York's Greenwich Village folk music scene of the 1950s and '60s. Also announced is a first venture into television, a quirky private eye series called *Harve Karbo* for Imagine Television.

## 2012

**6 February.** Filming begins in New York on *Inside Llewyn Davis* with Oscar Isaac, Justin Timberlake and Carey Mulligan.

Hailee Steinfeld on the set of *True Grit* (2010).

Ethan Coen and Joel Coen on the set of *True Grit* (2010).

# Filmography

## SHORT FILMS

### 'Tuileries'    2006
**Format** 35 mm. **Running time** 5 mins. With Steve Buscemi, Julie Bataille, Axel Kiener.

• Having made eye contact with a girl on the platform of a Paris Metro station, an American tourist is shocked when she kisses him to get her own back on her boyfriend. Segment from *Paris, je t'aime*.

### 'World Cinema'    1984
**Format** 35 mm. **Running time** 3 mins 20. With Josh Brolin, Grant Heslov, Brooke Smith.

• In an American cinema, a cowboy is hesitating between *The Rules of the Game* by Jean Renoir and *Climates* by Nuri Bilge Ceylan. Segment from *To Each His Own Cinema*, a French anthology film commissioned for the 60th anniversary of the Cannes Film Festival.

## FEATURE FILMS

### Blood Simple    1984
**Screenplay** Joel Coen, Ethan Coen. **Cinematography** Barry Sonnenfeld. **Production design** Jane Musky. **Editing** Roderick Jaynes, Don Wiegmann. **Music** Carter Burwell. **Producer** Ethan Coen. **Production** River Road Productions, Foxton Entertainment. **Running time** 1h 39. With John Getz (Ray), Frances McDormand (Abby), Dan Hedaya (Julian 'Greek' Marty), M. Emmet Walsh (Loren Visser).

• Convinced his young wife Abby has started an affair with barman Ray, Julian Marty hires private investigator Loren Visser to first photograph then murder the couple.

### Raising Arizona    1987
**Screenplay** Joel Coen, Ethan Coen. **Cinematography** Barry Sonnenfeld. **Production design** Jane Musky. **Editing** Michael R. Miller. **Music** Carter Burwell. **Producer** Ethan Coen. **Production** Circle Films, 20th Century Fox. **Running time** 1h 34. With Nicolas Cage (H. I. 'Hi' McDunnough), Holly Hunter (Edwina 'Ed' McDunnough), John Goodman (Gale Snoats), William Forsythe (Evelle Snoats), Trey Wilson (Nathan Arizona), Randall 'Tex' Cobb (Leonard Smalls).

• Unable to start a family, semi-retired thief Hi and retired cop Ed elect to steal one of the Arizona Quins born to a furniture tycoon. But their rash plan brings first prison escapees the Snoats brothers and then the Lone Rider of the Apocalypse to their door.

### Miller's Crossing    1990
**Screenplay** Joel Coen, Ethan Coen. **Cinematography** Barry Sonnenfeld. **Production design** Dennis Gassner. **Editing** Michael R. Miller. **Music** Carter Burwell. **Producer** Ethan Coen. **Production** Circle Films, 20th Century Fox. **Running time** 1h 55. With Gabriel Byrne (Tom Reagan), Marcia Gay Harden (Verna Bernbaum), Albert Finney (Leo O'Bannon), John Turturro (Bernie Bernbaum), Jon Polito (Johnny Caspar).

• In an unnamed East Coast city of the late 1920s, a turf war begins when Irish gangland boss Leo refuses to sell out a crooked bookie to his rival Johnny Caspar because he is the brother of his new girlfriend Verna.

### Barton Fink    1991
**Screenplay** Joel Coen, Ethan Coen. **Cinematography** Roger Deakins. **Production design** Dennis Gassner. **Editing** Roderick Jaynes. **Music** Carter Burwell. **Producer** Ethan Coen. **Production** Circle Films, Working Title. **Running time** 1h 56. With John Turturro (Barton Fink), John Goodman (Charlie Meadows), Judy Davis (Audrey Taylor), Michael Lerner (Jack Lipnick).

• In 1941 celebrated New York playwright Barton Fink is lured to Hollywood to write screenplays for Capitol Pictures. Afflicted with writer's block, he befriends a travelling insurance salesman from the hotel room next door – a man with a dark secret that will be unleashed as Barton recovers his muse.

### The Hudsucker Proxy    1994
**Screenplay** Joel Coen, Ethan Coen, Sam Raimi. **Cinematography** Roger Deakins. **Production design** Dennis Gassner. **Editing** Thom Noble. **Music** Carter Burwell. **Producers** Ethan Coen, Joel Silver (uncredited). **Production** Warner Brothers, Working Title. **Running time** 1h 51. With Tim Robbins (Norville Barnes), Jennifer Jason Leigh (Amy Archer), Paul Newman (Sidney J. Mussburger), Charles Durning (Waring Hudsucker), Bill Cobbs (Moses).

• In a fantastical New York of 1959, Waring Hudsucker, chairman of Hudsucker Industries, leaps to his death from the 45th floor of the Hudsucker Building. Conniving executive Sidney J. Mussburger hatches a plan to hire an idiot as their new chairman, sending the stock spiralling down, so he and the board can buy it up cheap. Fate, or perhaps God, will intervene when the chosen proxy Norville Barnes invents the hula hoop.

### Fargo    1996
**Screenplay** Joel Coen, Ethan Coen. **Cinematography** Roger Deakins. **Production design** Rick Heinrichs. **Editing** Roderick Jaynes. **Music** Carter Burwell. **Producer** Ethan Coen. **Production** PolyGram, Working Title. **Running time** 1h 38. With Frances McDormand (Marge Gunderson), William H. Macy (Jerry Lundegaard), Steve Buscemi (Carl Showalter), Peter Stormare (Gaear Grimsrud), Harve Presnell (Wade Gustafson).

• Deep in debt, Minnesotan car salesman Jerry Lundegaard hires two thugs to fake the kidnap of his wife in order for her rich father to pay the ransom. But as the plan slips out of control and the thugs turn killers, local police detective Marge Gunderson picks up the trail.

### The Big Lebowski    1998
**Screenplay** Joel Coen, Ethan Coen. **Cinematography** Roger Deakins. **Production design** Rick Heinrichs. **Editing** Roderick Jaynes, Tricia Cooke. **Music** Carter Burwell. **Producer** Ethan Coen. **Production** PolyGram, Working Title. **Running time** 1h 57. With Jeff Bridges (The Dude), John Goodman (Walter Sobchak), Julianne Moore (Maude Lebowski), David Huddleston (Jeffrey 'The Big' Lebowski), Steve Buscemi (Donny).

• In suburban Los Angeles, when Jeffrey 'The Dude' Lebowski is mistaken for a far richer Jeffrey Lebowski he is hurled unwittingly into a plot involving a stolen rug, the kidnap of his namesake's trophy wife, a missing ransom, an angry pornographer, a radical feminist artist and a band of German nihilists.

### O Brother,    1999
### Where Art Thou?

**Screenplay** Joel Coen, Ethan Coen. **Cinematography** Roger Deakins. **Production design** Dennis Gassner. **Editing** Roderick Jaynes, Tricia Cooke. **Music** T-Bone Burnett. **Producer** Ethan Coen. **Production** Touchstone, Studio Canal, Working Title. **Running time** 1h 46. With George Clooney (Ulysses Everett McGill), John Turturro (Pete), Tim Blake Nelson (Delmar).

• Based very loosely on *The Odyssey*, the story follows the trials of three idiots, led by Everett McGill, who abscond from a chain gang in Depression-era Mississippi. While pursued by the authorities, the trio go in search of buried treasure.

### The Man Who Wasn't There    2001

B&W **Screenplay** Joel Coen, Ethan Coen. **Cinematography** Roger Deakins. **Production design** Dennis Gassner. **Editing** Roderick Jaynes, Tricia Cooke. **Music** Carter Burwell. **Producer** Ethan Coen. **Production** Good Machine, Gramercy Pictures, Working Title, Mike Zoss Productions. **Running time** 1h 56. With Billy Bob Thornton (Ed Crane), Frances McDormand (Doris Crane), James Gandolfini (Big Dave Brewster).

• The year is 1949, and in order to fund an investment in a dry-cleaning business, introverted small-town barber Ed Crane tries to blackmail his wife's boss, with whom she is having an affair. The plan slips into murder, and his wife Doris ends up being accused of the deed.

### Intolerable Cruelty    2003

**Screenplay** Robert Ramsey, Matthew Stone, John Romano, Joel Coen, Ethan Coen. **Cinematography** Roger Deakins. **Production design** Leslie McDonald. **Editing** Roderick Jaynes. **Music** Carter Burwell. **Producers** Ethan Coen, Brian Grazer. **Production** Universal Pictures, Imagine Entertainment, Mike Zoss Productions. **Running time** 1h 40. With George Clooney (Miles Massey), Catherine Zeta-Jones (Marylin Rexroth), Cedric the Entertainer (Gus Petch), Billy Bob

Thornton (Howard D. Doyle), Geoffrey Rush (Donovan Donaly), Paul Adelstein (Wrigley).

• Top Los Angeles divorce lawyer Miles Massey, creator of an iron-clad prenuptial agreement, falls for his latest victim, Marylin Rexroth, a gold-digger who has an eye for a wealthy husband. Can they trust one another long enough to fall in love?

### The Ladykillers    2004

**Screenplay** Joel Coen, Ethan Coen. **Cinematography** Roger Deakins. **Production design** Dennis Gassner. **Editing** Roderick Jaynes. **Music** Carter Burwell. **Producers** Joel Coen, Ethan Coen. **Production** Touchstone Pictures, Mike Zoss Productions. **Running time** 1h 44. With Tom Hanks (Professor G. H. Dorr), Irma P. Hall (Marva Munson), J. K. Simmons (Garth Pancake), Marlon Wayans (Gawain MacSam), Tzi Ma (The General), Ryan Hurst (Lump Hudson).

• A remake of the 1955 Ealing comedy, in which a gang of Mississippi criminals plan to rob a riverboat casino via the cellar of an elderly widow. As she gets wise to their wrongdoing, the villains are dispatched, one by one, by their own ineptitude.

### No Country for Old Men    2007

**Screenplay** Joel Coen, Ethan Coen, adapted from the novel by Cormac McCarthy. **Cinematography** Roger Deakins. **Production design** Jess Gonchor. **Editing** Roderick Jaynes. **Music** Carter Burwell. **Producers** Joel Coen, Ethan Coen, Scott Rudin. **Production** Paramount Vantage, Miramax Films, Scott Rudin Productions, Mike Zoss Productions. **Running time** 2h 2. With Tommy Lee Jones (Sheriff Bell), Javier Bardem (Anton Chigurh), Josh Brolin (Llewelyn Moss).

• After finding a suitcase full of cash at the site of a drug deal gone horribly wrong, young hunter Llewelyn Moss goes on the run. On his tail comes an implacable hitman who will stop at nothing to complete his mission. And on the trail of them both comes the local sheriff.

### Burn After Reading    2008

**Screenplay** Joel Coen, Ethan Coen. **Cinematography** Emmanuel Lubezki. **Production design** Jess Gonchor. **Editing** Roderick Jaynes. **Music** Carter Burwell. **Producers** Joel Coen, Ethan Coen. **Production** Focus Features, Studio Canal, Relativity Media, Working Title, Mike Zoss Productions. **Running time** 1h 36. With John Malkovich (Osbourne Cox), Frances McDormand (Linda Litzke), George Clooney (Harry Pfarrer), Brad Pitt (Chad Feldheimer).

• After quitting his CIA analyst job, having been accused of a drink problem, Ozzie Cox begins his memoir, a disk of which accidentally gets left at Hardbodies gym. Discovering what they take for secret intelligence, gym employees Linda Litzke and Chad Feldheimer plan to sell their discovery to the Russians.

### A Serious Man    2009

**Screenplay** Joel Coen, Ethan Coen. **Cinematography** Roger Deakins. **Production design** Jess Gonchor. **Editing** Roderick Jaynes. **Music** Carter Burwell. **Producers** Joel Coen, Ethan Coen. **Production** Focus Features, Studio Canal, Relativity Media, Mike Zoss Productions, Working Title. **Running time** 1h 46. With Michael Stuhlbarg (Larry Gopnik), Richard Kind (Uncle Arthur), Fred Melamed (Sy Ableman), Sari Lennick (Judith Gopnik), Aaron Wolff (Danny Gopnik).

• Minnesota, 1967, and physics professor Larry Gopnik is up for tenure when his life starts to fragment. Larry seeks the council of three local rabbis.

### True Grit    2010

**Screenplay** Joel Coen, Ethan Coen, adapted from the novel by Charles Portis. **Cinematography** Roger Deakins. **Production design** Jess Gonchor. **Editing** Roderick Jaynes. **Music** Carter Burwell. **Producers**

Joel Coen, Ethan Coen, Scott Rudin. **Production** Paramount Pictures, Skydance Productions, Scott Rudin Productions, Mike Zoss Productions. **Running time** 1h 50. With Jeff Bridges (Rooster Cogburn), Matt Damon (LaBoeuf), Hailee Steinfeld (Mattie Ross), Josh Brolin (Tom Chaney), Barry Pepper (Lucky Ned Pepper).

• In 1870s Arkansas, fourteen-year-old Mattie Ross hires the services of Marshal Rooster Cogburn to go after the man who shot and killed her father. They are joined by Texas Ranger LaBoeuf as they enter the reservation from which the villain is reputed to have flown.

### PRODUCERS ONLY

### Down from the Mountain    2000
by Nick Doob, Chris Hegedus and D. A. Pennebaker

### Where the Girls Are    2003
by Jennifer Arnold and Tricia Cooke

### Bad Santa    2003
by Terry Zwigoff

### Romance and Cigarettes    2005
by John Turturro

# Selected Bibliography

Ronald Bergan,
*The Coen Brothers*,
London, Orion, 2000.

Josh Levine,
*The Coen Brothers*,
Toronto, ECW Press, 2000.

# Notes

**1.** Ronald Bergan, *The Coen Brothers*, Orion, 2000, p. 15.

**2.** The term 'film noir' was coined by French critic Nino Frank in 1946 to describe the rash of hard-boiled crime dramas coming out of Hollywood in the early 1940s and 1950s. They are marked by their emphasis on style, atmospheric black and white cinematography, and cynical world view. They would often centre on a central existential anti-hero – typically a private investigator. Such a stark outlook on humanity is considered to be the cumulative product of the American Depression, the horrors of World War II and Stalin's reign of terror.

**3.** Dashiell Hammett, *Red Harvest*, Crime Masterworks, Orion, 2003, p. 153.

**4.** Ronald Bergan, op. cit., p. 82; Josh Levine, *The Coen Brothers*, ECW Press, 2000, p. 25.

**5.** David Denby, *New York Magazine*, 21 January 1985, p. 51.

**6.** Pauline Kael, 'The Current Cinema: "Plain and Simple"', *The New Yorker*, 25 February 1985.

**7.** Josh Levin, op. cit., p. 44.

**8.** Ibid., p. 86.

**9.** Ronald Bergan, op. cit., p. 147.

**10.** 'Cast and crew interviews', *O Brother, Where Art Thou?*, Special Edition DVD, Momentum/Universal, 2000.

**11.** Ibid.

**12.** 'Commentary by Billy Bob Thornton and Joel & Ethan Coen', *The Man Who Wasn't There*, DVD, Entertainment, 2001.

**13.** Tom C. Smith, 'The Man Who Wasn't There – Twentieth Century Man', Metaphilm.com, 2 June 2003.

**14.** Peter Bradshaw, 'My Father Lived in Croydon', *The Guardian*, 15 June 2004.

**15.** John Patterson, 'We've killed a lot of animals', *The Guardian*, 21 December 2007.

**16.** Anthony Lane, 'Hunting Grounds', *The New Yorker*, 12 November 2007.

**17.** 'Finding the Burn – The making of Burn After Reading', *Burn After Reading*, DVD, Universal, 2008.

**18.** Shelia Roberts, 'Brad Pitt & Cast Interview, Burn After Reading', Moviesonline.ca, 2008.

# Sources

Collection Cahiers du cinéma: cover, inside front cover, pp. 2–3, 4–5, 6, 12, 13, 14, 15, 16, 17, 18–9, 21, 23, 26–7, 28, 29, 30–1, 33, 34, 35, 36–7, 40, 41, 42–3, 44, 46–7, 48–9, 54, 55, 70, 72–3, 74, 75, 76–7, 78, 79, 80, 81, 82, 85, 86–7, 89, 91, 92, 93, 94–5, 98 (3rd col.), 99, 100 (1st col., 2nd col., 3rd col. top and centre), 101 (2nd col. bottom, 3rd col.), 102, inside back cover.
Collection Cat's: pp. 20, 24, 38, 45, 52, 56, 60, 61, 62, 63, 64, 65, 66, 67, 68–9, 96–7, 101 (1st col., 2nd col. top).

Collection Christophel: pp. 50–1, 53, 88, 100 (3rd col. bottom).
Collection Photo 12: pp. 10, 58–9, 84.
Collection Rue des archives: pp. 8–9, 11, 98 (1st col., 2nd col.).
Screen grabs: p. 22.

# Credits

© Archives du 7e Art/DR: pp. 10, 58–9.
© Archives du 7e Art/Focus Features/ DR: p. 84.
© Circle Films: pp. 15, 16, 17, 100 (1st col. centre).
© Focus Features: pp. 70, 79, 80, 81, 82, 85, 86–7, 89, 91, 99 (3rd col.), 101 (3rd col. top and centre).
© Focus Features/Collection Christophel: p. 88.
© Good Machine International/Bac films: pp. 60, 61, 101 (1st col. top).
© Gramercy Pictures: pp. 38, 44, 45, 46–7, 48–9, 100 (3rd col. centre).
© Gramery Pictures/PolyGram Filmed Entertainment: pp. 2–3, 4–5, 40, 41, 42–3, 98 (3rd col.), 100 (3rd col. top).
© Mary Evans/Rue des archives: pp. 8–9, 98 (1st col.).
© Paramount Pictures: cover, inside front cover, pp. 55, 72–3, 74, 75, 76–7, 78, 92, 93, 94–5, 96–7, 99 (4th col.), 101 (2nd col. bottom, 3rd col. bottom), 102, inside back cover.
© River Road Production/Foxton Entertainment: pp. 12, 13, 14, 100 (1st col. top).

© Rue des archives/BCA: p. 11, 98 (2nd col.).
© Silver Pictures/Warner Bros/Working Title Films: pp. 34, 35, 36–7, 100 (2nd col. bottom).
© Touchstone Pictures/Gaumont Buena Vista International: pp. 66, 67, 68–9, 101 (2nd col. top).
© Touchstone Pictures/Universal Pictures: pp. 52, 54, 99 (1st col.).
© Touchstone Pictures/Universal Pictures/Collection Christophel: pp. 50–1, 53, 100 (3rd col. bottom).
© Twentieth Century Fox Film Corporation/Bac Films: p. 24.
© Twentieth Century Fox Film Corporation/Circle Films: pp. 6, 18–9, 20, 21, 22, 23, 26–7, 28, 29, 30–1, 33, 100 (1st col. bottom, 2nd col. top).
© Universal Pictures: pp. 62, 63, 64, 65, 101 (1st col. bottom).
© Universal Pictures/UIP: p. 56.

Opposite page: Ethan Coen, Joel Coen and Hailee Steinfeld on the set of *True Grit* (2010).
Cover: Javier Bardem in *No Country for Old Men* (2007).
Inside front cover: Josh Brolin in *No Country for Old Men* (2007).
Inside back cover: Josh Brolin in *No Country for Old Men* (2007).

**Cahiers du cinéma Sarl**
65, rue Montmartre
75002 Paris

www.cahiersducinema.com

First edition 2012 © 2012 Cahiers du cinéma Sarl

ISBN 978 2 8664 2903 4

A CIP catalogue record of this book is available from the British Library.

Series conceived by Claudine Paquot
Concept designed by Werner Jeker/Les Ateliers du Nord
Designed by Pascaline Richir
Printed in China